Praise

"Tennis provides a healthy lifetime activity the whole family can play together that teaches many valuable lessons. Here's a book every parent and coach will want for the tennis kid in their lives."
PAM SHRIVER, professional tennis player, television analyst, and tennis hall of famer

"There's no other book that explains many of the topics you cover."
DAVE, Tampa, FL, tennis parent

"Keith Kattan has done his homework. An invaluable head start for any parent or coach guiding the development of a young tennis player."
TONY LANCE, TENNIS magazine

"Raising Big Smiling Tennis Kids will help parents allow their children to play tennis for a lifetime. Very helpful."
PETER BURWASH, founder of PBI, the world's largest tennis management company, and author of Tennis for Life

"An excellent book for parents who want to get their children into tennis, I wish I'd had this book when I was a kid myself! As someone who has grown up with tennis as part of my life, I could have used a lot of this information."
ANDRE CHRISTOPHER, TENNIS WEEK magazine

"I want to tell you that your approach to this is one that I would and should follow to give my kids the best."
KEITH ADAMS, tennis-teaching professional

"Thank you for writing Raising Big Smiling Tennis Kids. Very easy to read and packed with information. Must-read for all parents of tennis kids"
GABRIELA, Las Vegas, NV, tennis parent

"A must read for any parent. Highly relevant and timely."
SEAN BRAWLEY, former player on the professional tennis tour who coaches athletes in tennis, football, and baseball

An Important Message to Our Readers

RAISING
Big Smiling Tennis Kids

A Complete Roadmap
For
Every Parent and Coach

Keith Kattan

Second Edition

Mansion Grove House

Raising Big Smiling Tennis Kids

ISBN 1932421114 **Second Printing 2006, Revised**

Published by Mansion Grove House. PO Box 201734 Austin TX 78720 USA.
Website: mansiongrovehouse.com
For information on bulk purchases, custom editions and serial rights: Email sales@mansiongrovehouse.com or write us, Attention: Special Sales.
For permission license including reprints, excerpts and quotes: Email permissions@mansiongrovehouse.com or write us, Attention: Permissions

Printed in the United States of America
Library of Congress Cataloging-in-Publication Data
Kattan, Keith.
Raising big smiling tennis kids : a complete roadmap for every parent and coach / Keith Kattan.-- 2nd printing 2006, rev.
p. cm.
Includes bibliographical references and index.
ISBN 1-932421-11-4 (pbk. : alk. paper)
1. Tennis for children. 2. Tennis for children--Coaching. I. Title.
GV1001.4.C45K38 2006
796.342083--dc22
2005031011

Editor: **Pamela Garrett** Permissions & Reviews: **Uday Kumar**
Cover Designers: **R. Christian Anderson** (Original Cover) & **Bill Carson** (Second Edition) Project Assistant: **Maureen Malliaras**

Credits:

- Dr. Seuss quote by permission of Dr. Seuss Enterprises, L.P.
- Robert Lansdorp quote by permission of TennisWizard.com.
- Raising the Bar, a portion of this section is excerpted from the April 2, 2001 issue of Business Week by special permission, copyright 2001 by The McGraw-Hill Companies, Inc.
- O'Connell's Ball Control Contest excerpted from the Nov 10, 2001 issue of ADDvantage by permission of United States Professional Tennis Association, and Dan O'Connell.
- References to Inner Tennis by W. Timothy Gallwey, copyright 1976 by W. Timothy Gallwey. Used by permission of Random House, Inc.
- Attributions to Dr. Jim Taylor from Positive Pushing: How to Raise a Successful and Happy Child by Dr. Jim Taylor. Copyright 2002 Dr. Jim Taylor. Reprinted by permission of Hyperion.
- Table 14.1 reprinted with permission of United States Tennis Court and Track Builders Association and the United States Tennis Association, from its Tennis Courts: A Construction and Maintenance Manual, Copyright 2001.

To

All tennis teachers.
My tennis kid, wife, and parents.
My happy-tailed companion – Buddy.

Contents

Common Acronyms

ASBA: American Sports Builders Association
ATP: Association of Tennis Professionals
ITF: International Tennis Federation
ITHF: International Tennis Hall of Fame
NFHS: National Federation of State High School Associations
NCAA: National Collegiate Athletic Association
PTR: Professional Tennis Registry
USTA: United States Tennis Association
USPTA: United States Professional Tennis Association
WTA: Women's Tennis Association

Introduction

"Before I got married I had six theories about bringing up children; now I have six children and no theories."
JOHN WILMOT, Earl of Rochester.

Tennis offers your kid unparalleled benefits – opportunities to travel the world, money for college, great career choices. Plus: friendship, character, and a lifetime of good health. Whether you know tennis or not; whether your kid is 2 or 18 and just starting, or has a few years of tennis experience, this book offers a complete roadmap to all the game has to offer. You'll find practical advice ranging from the best age to get your kid started in tennis, to pursuing a career in professional tennis.

Raising a child is not something you should learn as you go, especially if your kid is into sports. A wise man once said, "Experience is the worst teacher." After all, a child gives the parent one chance to get it right. We've all read about young players suffering injuries, poor coaching, burnout, money, and family problems. So, as a new parent myself, I decided to do my homework and find out the best way to introduce my young son to sports.

Years ago at graduate school, I was invited to work on an artificial intelligence (AI) system to help engineers predict the life of certain aging bridges. I was going to interview experts in the field and encapsulate their knowledge in a computer-based AI system. In a few months, the amount and variety of information I was gathering began to overwhelm my little computer-based rulebook and me.

I had a similar feeling of overload as I devoured numerous books and magazine articles on the subject of kids and sports and discussed what I learned with friends and family. However, I found that almost all the books focused on teaching the sport. The few exceptions that dealt with sports psychology, science, and nutrition were either academic or addressed the professional game. Media coverage included a few reports on sports parenting issues, but mostly the focus was on professional players and their biographies.

I dug deeper. Like needles in a haystack, hidden among coaching materials, scientific papers, and career profiles, I found answers to my questions, one by one: Why do kids pick one sport over another? As a tennis fan, I wondered how I could get my kid interested in tennis? What is the best age to start learning tennis? I know a coach in my neighborhood, how do I find out if he is right for my child? How about picking an appropriate racket and the right pair of shoes? What if, after the first lesson, my kid says he doesn't want to go back?

My kid enrolled in the neighborhood class. Fortunately, his coach turned out to be a wonderful influence. But my list of tennis parenting questions didn't stop there. As my kid's tennis years rolled by, I found myself asking, how much tennis is too much? At what age should kids start competition? Can sports injuries be avoided? What about college scholarships? How do players land sponsorship deals? Is professional tennis a good career option?

My quest continued, even as available information on these topics dwindled. I had one advantage: as owner of a small software company, work was hectic, but I could set my own hours. Instead of just dropping my kid off at his tennis lesson, I took the time to observe the class. Not just my kid, but also a variety of groups with different abilities.

I talked with coaches, other parents, and tennis administrators. I reflected on what works in junior tennis, sought expert corroboration when needed, and formed my own beliefs. The material for this book is drawn from those ten years of self-education as a tennis parent.

Tennis parenting poses unique challenges. Some parents feel that, for healthy development, a child should balance a variety of activities. Others believe that to achieve success, the child should be allowed to focus on one or two things. This book presents safe, practical steps to help you decide when and how to move from one parenting philosophy to another, depending upon your child's age, tennis proficiency, and level of interest.

I have focused much of my attention on unearthing the root causes of common sports parenting issues. For instance, we have been told over and over again, "Don't push kids." Rarely has anyone asked what motivates a well-meaning parent to push. Is pushing always bad? This book provides straightforward, non-judgmental answers to such questions, laying out step-by-step solutions to avoid common pitfalls.

The chapters Inside Tennis Organizations and Movers and Shakers give you the inside skinny on the business side of tennis. Knowing how the system works gives your kid an advantage. More importantly, that knowledge will fuel your involvement in growing the game. You owe it to your tennis kid.

"More info." This phrase, used throughout the book, will connect you to important websites and references. Linking this way makes the book an easy read while allowing access to thousands of pages of up-to-date and in-depth information and contacts.

The overriding emphasis of the book is to offer a complete and practical roadmap for the tennis parent and coach. If your kids are currently pursuing other sports, I hope this work inspires you to consider introducing them to tennis. I invite your thoughts on the usefulness of the book to you. I welcome suggestions for a future edition and would love to hear your success stories.

This book will empower you to raise kids who swing the tennis racket with as much aplomb as their happy smiles. I wish your tennis kid(s), and you, a joyous life.

Keith Kattan
Email: keith_kattan@mansiongrovehouse.com

1

Getting Kids Interested

"You make 'em, I amuse 'em."
DR. SEUSS, on the subject of raising children.

Little Johnny has a variety of sporting options next season – football, basketball, soccer, tennis, baseball, golf, and ice hockey. Mom encourages him to play two organized sports each season. Johnny tried football and soccer. He loved soccer and wants to sign up again. As his second sport, Mom is considering introducing him to tennis. There are many good reasons why tennis should be part of Johnny's repertoire.

Why Tennis? The Right and Wrong Reasons

Pretend you're a tennis novice. Ask any avid player why tennis is his primary sport. Quite probably you just pushed his hot buttons. Brace yourself for an eloquent, emphatic and, of course, endless exposé on the virtues of tennis.

His reasons will probably range from simple and sentimental to refreshingly innocent:

- *The simple:* Tennis is fun, easy, and offers fitness for life. Easy, as it takes just two to tango; social, as it takes at least two to tango. Tennis is truly a global sport and provides the opportunity to travel. It can also offer college scholarships and career opportunities. And tennis can play a big role in developing character and discipline.
- *The innocent:* Handle tennis competition well and you can handle anything life throws at you. The sport can be played on the cheap and is relatively safe because it's not a contact sport. Size doesn't matter and no child sits on the bench in tennis. A player can pick and choose tournaments in which to participate, unlike team sports with a fixed season schedule.
- *The sentimental:* Tennis bridges the family generation gap, as old and young can play together. Tennis brings together nice people from all walks of life.

But don't get all teary-eyed just yet. There are also some negative reasons for introducing a child to tennis, some very wrong reasons indeed. Prestige and prize money are valid motivators and their influence cannot be denied. However, playing solely for these external motivations takes the fun out of tennis and is a perfect recipe for burnout.

It's important to have counter-balancing, less materialistic motivators, too – love of the challenge, a desire to do one's best and give maximum effort. Nor should a child play merely for parental approval. Enthusiasm for a sport cannot be sustained if every loss is equated with letting the family down. Fortunately, there are specific steps described in this book that parents and coaches can take to ensure that a child develops positive, intrinsic motivations.

As a parent or coach, choosing to introduce your junior to tennis for all the right reasons, while excluding all the wrong ones, makes you part of a very special club – The Nice Tennis People Club. Welcome. You may now burst into tears.

Learn to Love the Game

Enjoying tennis yourself is a surefire way to jumpstart a child's interest. But even if you're new to tennis and your idea of a racket conjures up the Mafia, don't worry. You don't have to play to enjoy tennis.

For starters, invite a tennis friend over to watch a tournament on television. Have him explain the rules, basic strokes, and strategies. Stump him with questions like, why are the points love, 15, 30, 40 and game? A couple of drinks and your friend should come up with a memorable answer. Two or three more educational sessions with your tennis buddy and you may find yourself getting into the swing of things, so to speak. The point is, you can learn to love the game.

There may be initial stumbling blocks. Be persistent. Watch a few more tournaments on television. Read about the exciting life on the professional tennis circuit. "Venus Envy" by L. Jon Wertheim and "You Cannot Be Serious" by John McEnroe are just two of the books guaranteed to pique your passion.

Before you know it, you'll be picking up on all the excitement tennis has to offer. As you relax on the recliner, mesmerized by Andre Agassi's return-of-serves, in walks 4-year-old Johnny, who asks, "Dad, can I watch with you?" Voila!

A postscript to this fairytale ending is in order. Don't be surprised if after a few minutes of watching tennis your kid returns to his play dough. Remember, kids have short attention spans. However, when he does watch with you, patiently answer any questions he may have. Refrain from too much applause when your favorite player wins and from berating a player over a lost point.

Exposing Kids to Tennis

Enthusiastic parents are known to hang miniature rackets, balls, and balloons-that-don't-burst as crib toys to expose their babies to tennis. There are other, less extreme ways to teach a young child about tennis.

Watch a Group Lesson

The best way to jumpstart a young child's interest in tennis is by letting her watch a fun group lesson. Watching a tournament can also be fun, but a young child may prematurely, and often subconsciously, begin to place undue emphasis on winning and losing. And you never know when a player might get mad and throw his racket around or mutter "sweet-nothings" not intended for a young one's ears. This kind of stuff just sends the wrong message to a young spectator.

Instead, choose a group class where you know the kids are having fun. Take your child to watch five or six lessons. If an older sibling attends the class, this can be a convenient option. Plan to keep the young child engaged with off-court games, as her attention span is likely to be limited.

Learning by watching will give your child more confidence when she does get on the court. Observing a group lesson helps a young child realize the game is fun and that they too can learn to play. If all goes according to plan, your child will soon be asking to sign up.

Read Together

Tennis activity books and storybooks for preschoolers were published a few years ago, but are hard to find now. Try tennis catalogs and online bookstores. If you do find such books, reading stories and doing fun tennis-related activities like drawing and coloring with your child are great ways to spark a preschooler's curiosity about the sport. Someday, these shared moments will pay-off on the court.

A wider selection of tennis books is available for kids ages four to eight. Pass on titles that are biographical glorifications of tennis stars. Instead, focus on stories with a tennis theme and on titles that describe the rules of the game in an entertaining way.

Off-court Games

"It was a dark and stormy night. Two figures – one large and the other small, silhouetted by the chandelier, were on opposite ends of the dinner table. The two were blowing a ping pong ball back and forth across the table."

You probably guessed it by now. This is not a Stephen King excerpt, rather it's a description of a parent and child playing the game of Blow Out. Played indoors on any horizontal surface, Blow Out players aim to move a ping-pong ball toward the opponent by blowing hard on the ball in the opponent's direction.

Off-court games are a great way to introduce kids ages 4 and under to sports. There are plenty of fun games designed for young children that can help develop early skills suited for tennis.

Stork

Balance is crucial for tennis players. You can help develop your child's balance by playing this game. The player tries to balance standing on one leg with arms outstretched like a stork. Add a friendly challenge – see who can stork longer. The child is allowed to wobble if necessary, but the parent is not.

Medicine Ball

This game is designed to address the motor development patterns of children and develop a stronger foundation for tennis skills. Use a two to four-pound medicine ball. A soccer ball or a large sized koosh ball works, too. Two kids, approximately the same height, throw the ball to each other using a movement similar to the overhead service motion.

As the kids develop this skill, have them use a forehand groundstroke motion. Then reverse the motion and throw backhands.

Jump Rope

Jump roping can be fun and is good for timing and endurance. Look for adjustable ropes in durable plastic, with cushioned handles.

Juggle

Teaching kids to juggle is fun. Start with two small beanbags and, after a few weeks of practice, progress to three bags. Juggling is a great way to develop soft focus.

Z-Ball

You'll have your kids giggling and chasing the Z-ball in no time at all. This rubber ball has knobs on it, creating unpredictable bounces. The Z-ball is great for developing hand-eye coordination.

Being a Ballperson

Running down balls at a favorite star's match may be the most up-close-and-personal experience for a young ballperson. Sometimes, the player chooses to give the ballperson more than she bargained for – a winning ball or racket, for example; yeah, stars are humans too, you know. When that happens, be prepared for the inevitable barrage of bragging from the star-struck junior.

You don't need a professional tournament to get a young ballperson pumped up. Say a younger sibling is watching her brother at match-play practice. Offer the young girl some basic tips about pick-ups and watch her get about her job with gusto. You may have just handed the girl tickets to her tennis future.

Most tournament directors require ballperson hopefuls to be at least 10 years of age. Aspiring kids are trained in hand-eye coordination, footwork, throwing, and catching proficiency. They are offered one of two jobs: nets or backcourts.

When a player misses a shot or faults to end the point, it is the net-ballperson's job to run the ball down before it stops rolling. She then returns it to the backcourt-ballperson on the server side. A backcourter is trained to chase aces and return the ball to her counterpart on the server side.

Tennis Vacation

Pick a nice tennis resort and book a few kids' lessons with the hotel pro. Ask that the lesson be fun and relaxed. Mix in all the other fun activities the resort has to offer kids – the pool, a kids club, or perhaps a mini-circus. Your child is guaranteed to have a ball. More importantly, the child will identify tennis with all the other fun activities she enjoyed during the vacation.

Peter Burwash is a recognized tennis coach, winner of a number of international titles, and an author. He is best known for offering individual tennis programs at more than 60 of the world's finest tennis vacation sites. Select sites also host his entertaining PBI Tennis Show, which serves up an eclectic mix of music, amazing ball control demos, humor, and tennis tips (More info: pbitennis.com).

Travel agents aside, you can find books and websites specializing in tennis vacations. "World's Best Tennis Vacations", written by the popular travel writer, Roger Cox, is a useful guidebook for any tennis family. Cox also maintains an online guide (More info: tennisresortsonline.com) and contributes tennis travel articles to Tennis magazine (More info: tennis.com). These are all wonderful sources of information for planning your perfect tennis getaway. And, of course, the most fun-filled way to get your child started in tennis.

The First Coach

Selecting a coach is a parent's single most important job. You can learn about teaching professionals from tennis clubs, public recreation departments, and the two certifying organizations in the United States – the United States Professional Tennis Association (USPTA. More info: uspta.com) and the Professional Tennis Registry (PTR. More info: ptrtennis.org).

Over the years, a parent and child can find themselves choosing a coach at three phases of the junior's tennis development: the beginner phase, the development phase and the high performance phase. The first coach teaches the basics, the second oversees high school level competition, and the third prepares the junior for advanced competition at the regional and national levels, which may also include travel to tournaments.

Obviously, choosing the right coach in the beginner phase is crucial because this phase determines whether the junior will even want to play tennis. Besides, it's always easier to start with the right stroke mechanics, rather than hustling through the early years and having to do a lot of fix-its later.

In a club situation, don't worry too much about the head pro's or tennis director's qualifications. Make your decision based upon the coach that is actually going to teach *your* kid. There are specific qualities a parent can look for in order to find the right coach.

Certification

A good starting point is to find a coach who has earned credentials from either the USPTA or the PTR. USPTA certification is available in three levels, based upon years of teaching experience – Pro 1, 2, and 3. A Pro 1 certification means the coach has not only passed the proficiency test but also has the most years of experience. The PTR has a similar certification process. It certifies its members as Associate Instructor, Instructor, and Professional.

The Developmental Coach is another certification option. This is a non-career-path category for people who teach part time or coach high school teams. A Developmental Coach certification basically means the coach has attended a one-day workshop. These workshops are offered by the USPTA. The United States Tennis Association (USTA. More info: usta.com) is also in on the action, offering Developmental Coach workshops in conjunction with the USPTA and PTR.

The Developmental Coach credential is the easiest to earn, so at a minimum, look for a coach who has this credential. At the higher end of the spectrum, a USPTA Pro 1 or PTR Professional certification implies the individual is the best equipped to teach.

The USPTA recently introduced specialization paths for professionals who have attained Pro 1 level – Competitive Player Development, Little Tennis, Facility Management, and so on. A coach who has specialized training to teach children is a big plus.

In addition, both the USPTA and PTR have continuing education workshops so a coach can stay up-to-date.

Making It Fun

If you remember only one keyword for raising a successful tennis kid, remember this one – "Fun." The ability to make a class fun is the most important qualification for a child's first coach. The coach should be able to communicate with kids lightheartedly, using analogies to explain shots and techniques. For example, a coach might explain the volley shot using the "high-five" gesture.

Say, you have to decide between a Pro 1 coach who conducts his class with a serious poker face, or a less qualified Developmental coach who uses fun and games to engage the kids. Your choice is clear – pick the coach who makes it the most fun. As long as a kid is having a good time, self-motivation and tennis development occur naturally.

A child is likely to have fun not only as a result of the way a coach teaches but also in response to his attitudes. Look for enthusiasm – someone who believes in rewarding effort as much as outcome, creating an environment that encourages trying new skills, and who has thc ability to focus on a particular child, even in a group situation.

The only way to make a good assessment is to watch the coach's group lessons. Shortlist a few prospects and watch their classes. Ideally, pick a three to four week period and watch two or three lessons coached by each prospect. Include your child. This time invested up-front is more than worth every hour. After all, that first coach will determine whether your child gets in the game or not.

Parent as Coach

A professional coach, after attempting to teach his son, stepped off the court and vented his frustration by whispering to no one in particular, "I don't think I can handle him on court anymore. He is just not interested in tennis." Parenting kids and coaching them are two of the most challenging roles any adult will ever face. Naturally being a parent-coach makes it the toughest assignment of all.

It's understandable that a parent who is a professional coach or proficient player would want to teach his own child. After all, who better to assess the child's abilities and moods? Experts caution against taking on this dual role, especially once a child outgrows his pre-teen years. By then, parenting alone becomes a challenging task, and the competition phase can make the relationship between a coach and student an emotional powder keg.

As a parent, if you choose to coach your own child because you want to, or because no other coach is available, or to save money on lessons, it's best to limit your coaching to the beginning phase. When it's time for lessons, go with the mindset of *playing* with your child rather than teaching him tennis. Young children play sports for fun; learning is simply a by-product. Keep this simple truth in mind and you'll be your child's best coach ever.

Whether you choose to teach tennis to your child or not, remain actively involved in the early years. Be a regular practice partner or feed balls to help practice what the pro has taught. Don't assume you can just turn your child over to a great pro and get him hooked. Children need to experience an emotional involvement if they are to choose tennis as the sport of a lifetime. A good parent is clearly best qualified to offer the young child memorable tennis experiences.

2

First Class

"I decided that I want to live the rest of my life happy with what I'm doing."
MONICA SELES, professional tennis player.

Many a would-be Agassi, or Capriati, and thousands of recreational prospects, have been lost to the future of tennis just because that first class was not appropriately designed for the little beginner. You just have to watch a beginner session to be convinced.

Consider a 4-year old and a 10-year old, who have never been exposed to tennis. Both will be wielding the racket for the first time, joining a so-called beginner group of 8-year olds who have been playing a few years. Add to this mix a first lesson drilling forehand, backhand, and volley techniques. Chances are, before long, either the 4-year old or the 10-year old, or worse both, will drop out, disappointed because they were unable to keep up.

The first few classes are so critical they ought to be included in an initiation level, separate from the traditional beginner, intermediate, and advanced. The initiation session can run for six to eight classes, after which kids advance to the beginner level. The initiation session should include first-timers of roughly the same age, even if the group musters only two kids.

The Right Age

Ask any coach or expert the ideal age to get your kid started in tennis and you're guaranteed to get responses that are all over the map. Some may say 3 years old, while others opine that ages 6 to 9 are perfect. Then there's the politically correct expert who answers, "Whenever your child is ready." Thanks for the advice, you say.

The really smart experts are those who pretend they've suddenly gone stone deaf. Because, in fact, when a parent poses the "right-age" question, what he really means is, "What is the ideal age to get my kid started in tennis *so he can win Wimbledon*?" And that, as they say, is the root of all trouble.

Jumpstart Interest

Common sense dictates that a kid has to have basic comprehension and motor skills before considering any sport. That's about 3 years old. After that, you can use gentle and innocuous methods to jumpstart their interest in tennis and begin to test the level of their interest.

There are simple ways to introduce kids to tennis. Read a tennis picture book; play a paddle game or catch game with a foam ball; explain a tennis match on television; enjoy a picnic that includes attending a local tournament; or visit a tennis club. A few of these jumpstart sessions and you're ready to gauge your child's interest in the sport.

Most parents have a system of rewards for good behavior. Ask your kid if he would like to earn a junior tennis racket for being good. Suggest a visit to the court to play crazy-catches. Pay attention if your child voluntarily watches a televised match with you and seems to enjoy it. If interest fails to develop, try to jumpstart the process again a few months or even a year later. If your kid is destined to take up tennis, he will eventually show interest. When that happens, you know you've found the right age.

Right Goal, Right Way

"My son is 18, is it too late to get started in tennis?" The answer is yes, and no. Yes, if his goal is to win 15 Grand Slam events and top Pete Sampras‘ record. No, if the goal is to join a club and win a local tournament. At 16, making the college team may be an attainable goal.

At 13, perhaps winning on the Sectionals circuit is possible. Beginning tennis at age 11 means a good shot at the Nationals. Starting at age 9 or earlier, with hard work, the Pro circuit and a Grand Slam are clear possibilities. See the point? Almost every age is right for the child, provided the goal is adjusted accordingly. At every level, a child has the opportunity to reach for the pinnacle. Once a kid achieves it, he can choose to challenge himself at the next level.

For every age there is also a right way to introduce tennis. For a 3 to 5 year old, simply playing munchkin games is a great start. Munchkin games build interest, hand-eye coordination, and footwork. Kids 6 to 12 years old, and who are just beginning, can get started with a ralleyball format, which encourages team participation and is played on a short-court (More info: usta.com). Over time, students can use the full court. Kids who are 13 and older can get started with traditional skill development lessons. A few follow-up practice matches later and they'll be ready to try out for their first tournament.

So instead of asking what age is the right one to get started, pose the question differently. My kid is such-and-such years old, what would be an appropriate tennis goal for him to set? Just as importantly, what is the best way to get him started toward achieving that goal?

The Right Class

The importance of a child's first tennis lesson can never be over emphasized. Get it right the first time, the kid will come back for the next lesson and the next. Before long, the child will take up tennis as a lifetime sport. On the other hand, attempt to teach backhand stroke and hone the service motion in the first class and, chances are, the kid will turn to another sport.

Initiation Classes

Forget about hand-eye coordination, footwork, and forehand technique. The initiation classes have one objective: get the kids to come back for the next ones. Tell jokes, play games, even those apparently unrelated to tennis skills, and think up excuses to hand out candies.

Do whatever it takes to keep them giggling during the 30 minutes or so. Accomplishing this over the next few classes does more for the little one's tennis development than any instruction in hand-eye coordination, footwork, or stroke technique.

Group Composition is Critical

Class composition depends on the type of tennis instruction, of course, whether it's recreational, group, private, or semi-private. Recreational programs are run at camps and free-for-alls designed to expose a lot of kids to tennis. Recreational tennis classes might have as few as 9 and as many as 30 kids, of all ages.

Group classes have up to eight children of roughly equal ability who progress together, class by class. Kids love to learn in groups. But the downside is that in a class that emphasizes skill, by the third session or so, children show dramatic differences in progress – something experts say should be avoided like a disease. By the end of the series of group classes, many kids feel left behind and there are only one or two who want to come back for the next series. Group classes work best when kids have already been exposed to tennis and demonstrate roughly equal ability.

Private lessons – one-on-one sessions with an experienced professional – can cost as much as $30 to $80 an hour but may be worth it for kids whose primary objective is to improve as quickly as possible. It is common for intermediate-to-advanced level kids to intersperse private lessons with group drills.

Semi-private lessons start with two to three kids in a similar age and ability group. Rich Maizel, Managing Partner at New Shrewsbury Racquet Club in Tinton Falls, New Jersey, says that taking semi-private lessons is the best way for a beginner to get going. "It tends to be more fun for beginners who have a lot to learn and then you have a buddy to practice with as you both get better," says Maizel. In fact, a semi-private class with all first-timers is the best way to go.

Parents should insist that the initiation session have only first-timers of roughly the same age. Often a new kid is entered in a class of the same age group, but the other children have been playing for a year or two. In other cases, a group of all first-timers is formed, but the kids are of different ages. In both instances, the new kids, especially the very young ones, come off the court feeling frustrated and disappointed because they can't coordinate as well as others in the supposedly all-beginner class.

In spite of disparities in skill and age, an experienced professional may be able to work with a new kid so that he or she doesn't feel inadequate. But, as a parent, it's best not to take chances. Give your kid the best opportunity to take up tennis. Start in a semi-private group with kids who are all first-timers and of roughly the same age.

Class Format

Even in a small first-timers-only group, the emphasis should be on fun and group games. Parents new to tennis may find the initiation strategy unconventional. An irate parent might demand money back, because no "tennis" was taught in the class. To avoid this situation, coaches can incorporate a question-and-answer session with parents as a part of the first class. A typical format might include:

- Coach–parent conference: Discuss initiation class objectives
- Stretches
- Coach–student conference: Q-and-A about court etiquette

- Games
- Cool downs
- Rewards to all kids: Popsicles, juices, and treats are great. Take-home stuff like stickers and foam balls are sure to send them home smiling and eager to return for the next class.

When kids leave with beautiful feelings associated with being on the court, the first class is a success.

The Games Approach

In the games approach kids learn by playing tennis games and discovering skills and strategies along the way. The approach itself is now old news, albeit a perfectly valid method of teaching.

In an earlier technique-based approach tennis is taught as skills first, strategy next, and play last. Kids learn the basic skills first – forehand, backhand, and serve. Each skill is practiced by repetitive drilling. The kids are then allowed into match play. Most beginners, however, are unable to mimic the newly acquired skills in a match situation. This is because they have only been taught how to hit a particular stroke and not when and why to use it in a match situation.

Coaches use a combination of both approaches. The games approach works best for Initiation and Beginner levels. Let's face it, a young child attends a tennis clinic not to *learn* tennis but to *play* the game. As the child develops rally consistency, the technique-based approach is appropriate to teach advanced techniques.

Nicole den Duyn, an educational sports consultant, suggests a sequence of steps in the games approach (More info: Select References 1):

1. Game
2. Game appreciation: Time should be given for players to see what the game is all about and why we need rules for a good game.
3. Tactical awareness: Problem solving is a critical approach to teaching games for understanding.
4. Decision-making: What to do and how to do it.
5. Skill execution: This is assessed individually.
6. Performance

Here are some examples of familiar games with a games-approach twist for kids at the initiation level (More info: Select References 2):

Game 1: Around the World

Eight students on each court with four on opposite sides. A large soft ball. Throw the ball over the net with both hands. After one bounce the student at the other end catches it and throws it back. After throwing, run around to the back of the opposite court.

Questions:

Where should you target the ball?
Where should you best position yourself to receive the ball?

Game 2: Ralleyball

Stand in pairs on a short court up to service line. Play a mini-game with a foam ball. First with one bounce of the ball allowed and then without a bounce. Encourage students to design their own rules such as calling out scores when serving.

Questions:

Where should you throw the ball to score a point?
Where should you position yourself to receive the ball?
If a player were at the back of the court where would you throw the ball and what is the name of the throw you would use?
If the player were at the front of the court what is the name of the throw you would use?

When kids understand what to do in a game, they want to develop the skills to play the game. The coach can then demonstrate those skills: practice using game-like drills and individually identify player errors, thus helping to correct them.

The keys to the games approach are the questioning technique, games-guided discovery of rules and techniques, and problem solving. Most important is the emphasis on games and fun.

Once a Week

Usually children start out with weekly classes. Even though a child has enjoyed his first class, children being who they are, he may require extra effort from a parent to get him to the next class. After a few successful classes a child gets in the groove and, given a choice, may want to play more often.

In the initiation phase less is more. Take the case of the San Jose woman whose children loved their weekly class so much they began clamoring for more, asking for two classes each week. The mom, proficient in tennis herself, played twice a week in a tennis league. Invoking reverse-psychology, the mom had her kids accumulate a certain number of good-behavior points over a two-month period – doing their homework, tidying up their rooms, etc. Needless to say, the mom received a lot of mileage from the kids' interest in tennis. After two months the children earned their way to more tennis – a weekly day-at-the-court with mom in addition to the regular once a week lesson.

Robert Lansdorp coached Tracy Austin, Pete Sampras, and Lindsay Davenport. Talking about the schedule of his illustrious protégés as they started in tennis, the coach says, "You can name every single player with whom I have worked. They had no more than an hour, sometimes two hours a week."

Finding a Court

Okay, so your six-year old is all excited after his first tennis class. Now it's the weekend and he can't wait to have some fun with you on the court. It's the 21st century, we ought to be able to flip open our mobile phone or personal digital assistant, select the "Find-a-Court" menu and, based on a GPS reading of location, receive a listing of nearby courts.

Well, at least we ought to be able to do that. Some companies are making brave attempts to introduce just such find-a-court services for the web, phone, and PDAs. But until they figure out how to make money from it and until their databases are comprehensive and up-to-date, let's just do a little web surfing or let our fingers do the walking through the yellow pages of the phone book.

Check out your local public courts. There are thousands of such courts throughout the country, built and maintained by city or county recreation departments. A majority of these courts are free and open to the public throughout the day. Always honor the posted playing time limits when others are waiting.

Some recreation departments have reservation systems for certain courts. The day-use fees are usually inexpensive, about $1 to $5 per hour. Lighted courts can run as high as $25 an hour. Reserving

An Open Letter

Dear Coach:

I am writing you from Ixtapa, set on the Pacific coast of Mexico. Don't feel too sorry for me, because between the beautiful beach, lovely wife, and a golden kid – life couldn't get any better.

Right now, perched on the patio of this beautiful Hacienda-style villa with a laptop and overlooking a glowing sunset horizon, I reflect on your coaching years with me and feel grateful for the wonderful education.

But before I get all soap-operaish and disappear into the sunset, I decided to put down my tennis wish list, addressed to you and other coaches working with kids:

- Coach-parent conference: Before the start of a new session, include a 10-minute Q&A with all parents discussing objectives, methods, and etiquette.
- Invite parents to participate in feeding balls, leading footwork drills and so on. Work together with parents to form a positive coaching alliance.
- Incorporate a thorough 5-to-10 minute stretching session at the beginning and end of each class. Better still, make warm-up and cool-down something kids look forward to with funny talk and games!
- In each class, impart mental conditioning techniques such as coping with losing, learning to win, and how to focus.

I thank the coaching community, and you, for the yeoman service to all future stars.

Regards,

Your Student, Who's Also A Parent

a court is useful, especially when holding community events.

Occasionally, public courts are crowded or poorly maintained resulting in floor cracks and torn nets. To control usage, public courts like the Monterey Tennis Center charge an annual access fee of $200 for unlimited use of its six courts. The fee assures well-maintained courts and adequate court time. Also included are many of the perks of a private tennis club: ball machines, a certified coach, and pro shop. On the whole, public courts can be a totally adequate place to get a kid started in tennis.

Also check out the courts at schools and colleges. They are usually well maintained and almost all are open to the public when students and staff are not using them. Many apartment complexes have tennis facilities, some even have resident tennis pros.

Private tennis clubs (More info: ihrsa.org) and the YMCA and YWCA are good places to find reservable courts. They also have great auxiliary features like pools and fitness rooms. When your kid begins to get serious about tennis, membership in one of these clubs may be worth the cost.

Finding a Backboard

There are lots of ways to find courts, but there will be times when you go out with your kid and can't find a place to play. It's one of those days – your club courts are all filled up and nearby public courts are over crowded. The last thing you want is a 6-year-old pumped up to whack balls and nowhere to go.

Develop a backup plan. Use off-court games and drills to keep your kid enthused. Better yet, identify a tennis backboard in a nearby park that the little one can hit against. If that's not available look for a hitting wall, found at many schools. There are numerous drills and games you can play against a hitting wall. Just tape up a net line about three feet high, remember to shorten that backswing, and you're ready to go.

When no hitting surface is at your disposal, consider a Rebound Net. These portable 7-foot by 7-foot frames with a net that rebounds balls at various speeds and angles is perfect for practicing on the go – on or off the court. It weighs just 15 pounds and can be set up on any smooth surface: home driveway, cul de sac, gymnasium, or backyard.

Practicing with Peewees

When famous cellist Pablo Casals was asked why, at the age of 85, he continues to practice five hours a day, he replied, "I have the notion I am making progress." Practice is just as important as lessons. It can be a real source of enjoyment and an end in itself.

Schedule a practice session with your child and make it a regular activity, something you'll both look forward to. Use the same techniques and games introduced during the lessons. If you cannot be present during lessons, speak with the coach or have him provide a written lesson-plan so you know what he's worked on.

Practicing with peewees requires a lot of patience, but sessions should go a lot smoother when you use the games approach. If you have a question about or disagreement with something the coach has told your child, don't contradict him in front of your child. Speak with the instructor privately.

Try role-playing. Ask your child to pretend to be the coach and you his student. Both you and the child are guaranteed loads of fun. Always highlight accomplishments, not mistakes. And remember, while the coach teaches tennis skills, you are the teacher of things far more important – attitude, character, and life skills.

3

In the Groove

"I figure practice puts your brains in your muscles."
SAM SNEAD, professional golfer.

A 10-year-old who receives motivation from a coach to learn, and support from a parent for practice, will grow into a 16-year-old who is more likely to be still hitting balls and enjoying it. Encouragement from and involvement by grown-ups helps kids get in the groove.

Getting Kids Hooked

Two words: parental involvement. There are many famous examples, including all of the US Open mens' champions going back 20 years: Pete Sampras, Lleyton Hewitt, Marat Safin, Andre Agassi, Patrick Rafter, Stefan Edberg, Boris Becker, Mats Wilander, Ivan Lendl, John McEnroe, and Jimmy Connors. Without exception, all these men recall their early years, when a mom or dad was involved in their tennis.

The stories are part of tennis folklore – parents who never played tennis but did all they could to support their kids. Mike Agassi built a backyard court with his own hands for his son; Dad Lleyton had one built for junior. Karl-Heinz Becker hired a coach to teach 8-year-old Boris, but not before designing the famous Baden Tennis Center across the street from his home.

Georgia and Sam Sampras fed young Pete and sister Stella balls because they couldn't afford lessons. Some champions had tennis bloodlines. Gloria Connors rolled balls to a swinging Jimmy at a club where she worked as a teaching pro. Olga Lendlova and Rausa Safin were top ten players who hitched their to-be-famous namesakes for hitting sessions.

Feeding balls to a child; playing games taught in a lesson; encouraging the child to hit off a backboard; enjoying recreational play with a bunch of neighborhood kids; or simply watching an exciting match on television can all be great motivators for a child.

When a Mom and Dad who have never played tennis before take tennis lessons, begin to play tournaments, and return from the club smiling and content, it sends a message to the kids that tennis is fun to learn and to play. A non-playing parent can also get involved by volunteering at a community tennis association. Anything a parent does to get connected to tennis is sure to spark the child's interest.

The bottom line is, lessons alone will not get a kid hooked on tennis. Practicing with a parent and developing a family connection to tennis will. Whether or not the parent is a tennis player is not important; what matters is involvement beyond paying for lessons and dropping kids off at the courts.

Learn to Handle Loss

At a parent-teacher conference for second-graders, the teacher was asked how parents could help their kids. The wise teacher replied, "Play a lot of games with your kids and play so they lose."

Why is it important to learn to handle loss? Face it, in a draw of 64, the odds are heavily stacked against a player. In singles elimination 63 players are destined to lose. There's no guarantee that the player who wins will win again the next time. In an individual sport like tennis, the player is solely responsible for the match result – fair and square. A loss not handled well can weigh heavily on a junior's self-esteem and enjoyment of the game.

Fear of Losing

"My father," Chris Evert has said, "taught me one important lesson: to not be afraid to lose." The best way to remove the fear of failure is to de-emphasize wins and losses, especially in the early years. That means don't over-celebrate a child's wins, and don't go ballistic after a loss. In either case, compliment the child's effort and ask, "What did you learn today?" Be genuine about it; a child can see through cover-ups faster than you can say game, set, match.

The Three Step Solution

Any junior can follow this three-step process in order to handle a loss without feeling like a loser:

✓ Handshake: Shake hands with the opponent after every match, regardless of the result.

✓ Cope with losing: It's okay to be disappointed and a little hurt. After all, a lot of lessons, practice, and effort are invested and every child copes differently. Some sulk, others verbalize, still others take their minds off a loss by playing a video game or watching television.

A parent should let the child work it out. It may be best to simply make a perfunctory remark or two and stay out of it.

✓ Find redeemable qualities in a lost match: Losing doesn't destroy self-esteem; the lack of ability to find redeemable qualities in a lost match does. Did you play your best? Did you stay relaxed? Were you focused on the point at hand? Did you improve first-serve percentage? Did you put into play the passing shot you had practiced? Did the match help improve your ranking points? If so, you're a winner.

None of these things come easily or naturally to an eight-year old who's just lost her first match. That's why it's important for parents and coaches to teach young players to handle losses, the earlier the better. Admittedly, there will be times when the child bursts into tears after losing an important match. Relax. Wait a day or two, and reinforce the three steps again.

Reward Effort

In many junior team sports, all players are awarded prizes for their participation and effort, regardless of a match's result. This is a great practice and ought to be incorporated into all under 12s tennis tournaments, because this is the age when children are still learning to cope with losing.

Far from rewarding mediocrity, explaining why every player deserved an award, even though some may have lost matches, helps kids learn to measure accomplishments in improvements and effort rather than simply in wins and losses. Besides, in a sanctioned tournament players are motivated to win anyway because they earn ranking points.

Parent-child Practice

Handling a loss can be practiced in an emotionally safe environment. A parent-child session is as safe as it can get. The objective is for the child to practice match play with a bigger, better player, learn to handle loss, and find ways to improve.

First, promise you *will not* say, "Johnny, let's go hit some balls and I'll teach you how to lose." You're going to be subtler than that, or perhaps you'll simply keep the game plan to yourself. Admit it – it's frightening to face your 10-year-old across the net, knowing you're about to beat him. So remember to carry Johnny's favorite Jelly Belly. You'll need it.

Match play is appropriate when the junior can rally consistently. Develop a handicap system so you don't have to give the match away to make junior feel good. Jennifer Yoder, a teaching pro who often practices with her 11-year-old, uses her own handicap system for parent-child match play.

"I play sets with my kid," says Jennifer, "The rules are the parent is allowed only first serves and cannot hit aces or winners. In the beginning my son lost 6-0. Of course, I de-emphasized the result; rewarded his effort; helped him find improvements in his game; and set a modest goal for the next match – win one more point than the previous set. And I kidded him. Guess what, I'm better than you. After a year or so, he is now doing 6-3. The best part – he is fine with it and having fun running down balls and giving it all he can."

The Four-Ball Winner is another perfect handicap game that rewards keeping the ball in court. "One of our family favorites is the Four-Ball Winner," writes Lawrence Tabak in Tennis magazine. "This is played like regular tennis except that the child wins every point in which the adult, who isn't allowed to hit any winners, is forced to hit a fifth shot. It is an easy game to handicap – make it 3, 6 or 10 shots, so that as the child improves it becomes even more challenging for the parent."

Other common handicapping methods are awarding a 30-love advantage in a game, a two-love lead in a set, and allowing the junior to serve from the service line. Pick a formula that will allow him to compete hard. Reward effort.

Learning by Watching

Walking, running, opening doors, and climbing stairs - a child learns new things everyday just by watching Mommy and Daddy. Now replace Mommy (just for a little while!) with a Vic Braden tennis teaching video. Can a child learn the game watching a video? An interesting thought, though it's doubtful tennis players can sufficiently develop this way alone.

Training Videos

Tennis involves more complex human motions than an exercise like walking. There is a lot more to tennis than just repetitive motion – strategy, for example. But we know many recreational players study training videos and picture books and become pretty good competitors. Richard Williams picked up just enough of the basics from videos to get his famous daughters started on tennis. Training videos can be great teaching aids for juniors as well by breaking down a stroke frame by frame.

Fortunately, parents, junior coaches, and even beginning junior players can find a good choice of videos developed by masters like Stan Smith, Vic Braden, Nick Bollettieri, Tom Avery, and John Yandell. These tennis videos can help a coach become better and a junior perfect strokes, correct common mistakes, and hit consistently. Videos can help even a non-playing parent appreciate what the coach is teaching and understand how the child is performing technically.

Television

Try this experiment. Let your kid watch a stockcar race on television for about an hour. Immediately head to the garage with your junior and, without actually starting the car, plonk him on the drivers' side of the parked car. Guess what? More than likely, he'll make an aggressive go at the steering wheel just like he watched the drivers do on television.

On a less dangerous note, get the junior interested in watching an exciting professional tennis match on television. Children learn by subconscious absorption of visual images, so they don't need much explanation.

In addition to keeping an eye on the score and the glamorous celebs in the stands, it's fun to watch while pretending to be doing a scouting report. Key portions of the match worth paying attention to include:

- When and how often the player gets to the net.
- Receiver's position at the baseline and reaction.
- Play during key games: tiebreaker, game following a 3-all score, game after a break, and set games.
- Comments from the experts.

To learn from watching televised matches one has to be an active, thinking participant in the game. Once again, remember that young children have extremely limited attention spans, so don't be surprised or annoyed when your junior wanders in and out of the television room.

Tournaments

Some people swear by the aura created by a front row seat at a professional tournament. Others prefer the close-ups and ball taps as seen and heard on high-definition television. The front rows offer nuances that cannot be seen on television. Speed of serve and rallies, for instance. Height of the ball over the net, wicked bounces from a spin, or a kick serve all come alive from the baseline vantage point.

But tennis aside, soaking up the hustle and bustle of a tournament can be a wonderful family experience. On a lucky day, Maria Sharapova will sign the big autograph ball your little girl reaches out to her as the diva heads for the locker room.

Effective Practice

Grown ups practice to improve, kids practice to have fun. Understand this and there should be no problem getting your 10-year-old to the practice courts.

Make a Plan and Stick to It

Practice with a purpose may be an overused phrase, but it is so true. Practicing without a plan encourages players to repeat only their best shots, overlooking all the weaknesses of their game. In the beginning practice the drills and games taught in class. Once the junior has begun playing tournaments, have the coach suggest a plan to enhance strengths and improve weaknesses.

Stick to the practice plan. During Pete Sampras‘ junior years he switched from a two-handed backhand to a single-handed backhand. The coach felt the two-handed stroke was limiting Pete’s reach. It took Pete nearly a year of practice to develop competency in the new technique. During the year he was not afraid to use it in competition, even though he lost matches because of it. But he stuck to his guns…or shall we say to his pistol.

Practicing a weak stroke for a few days does little to improve the stroke during a match. Repeat the new stroke technique until it is built into muscle memory. Experts suggest concentrating on a problem area for at least a two-week period. Let’s say the coach has suggested improvements are needed in the serve. Practice 30 to 40 serves each session, and try it in match play and tournaments during this period as well.

How Much, How Often?

Given a kid's limited attention span, it's best to limit practice sessions to 40 to 60 minutes with frequent breaks. In any case, stop while the kid is still interested.

No one can say how often to practice. Basically, the more hours of effective practice one puts into tennis, the more one gets out of it. But be wary of repetitive motion injuries. Every player has to come up with his own practice schedule based on goals, commitment, and level of interest.

Some coaches say a junior who wants to begin competing in sanctioned tournaments within the year may need about four to six hours of court time per week. This includes private lessons, group clinics, and practice sessions. So if a child is taking one hour of private lessons and another two hours of group clinics, keep the practice time to about one to three hours each week.

Practice Program

Parents often have to come up with creative ways to make a drill fun and, at the same time, achieve a specific objective. Here are guidelines from the professionals that will make practice effective and interesting:

- Five factors: Strokes are not the only techniques that must be learned. Practice footwork, agility, mental toughness, and strategy.
- Strong and weak points: Pete Sampras practiced his strong serve as well as the single-handed backhand – his nemesis at that time.
- Over-practice: Give it all during practice and you're bound to do the same in a match. Once again, be wary of injuries by limiting over-practice to short periods. Experts also advise not to over-practice the day before a match.
- Incorporate mental elements: Simulate tough match situations and practice playing in a relaxed and focused state. The score is 3-all and the player is serving the all-important seventh game.
- Spice it up: Experts have developed a number of munchkin games to make practice fun. "Munchkin Tennis" by Jack Hutslar and "Tennis for Kids" by Reggie Vasquez Jr., are great resources. The USPTA has dedicated an entire website to making practice fun for little kids (More info: littletennis.com).

- Specific short-term goals: Develop goals that are process-oriented rather than overly results-oriented. Instead of starting with a first-serve percentage as a short-term goal, set goals for perfecting the toss.

Measuring Progress

"Great, yesterday you got 6 out of 15 serves in, today you did eight. That's wonderful improvement. Good work, Johnny." This may sound like positive, encouraging feedback. But for a junior, especially one under 12 who is there to have fun, the emotional plodding drill after drill can be exhausting.

When you were a kid how would you have liked it if your teacher prepared a daily report card for you and discussed weaknesses and strengths with you every single day? By all means monitor your child's progress from practice to practice, but do it discreetly.

A parent's primary role at practice is to reinforce the coach's suggestions and gently help make fixes to a technique, not be a judge of results. Discuss observations with the coach, not with your child, especially the under 12s. Let the coach figure out how and when to move the child to the next level.

Record observations on-court or immediately after practice in a workbook or electronic handheld device. If you love gadgets use the tennis match data recorders you wear like a wristwatch to collect statistics on-court and download the records to a computer for analysis.

Practice Partner

Until a child can sustain short rallies, it's best for her to practice with a parent. Scout other family members, the neighborhood, and local school and college teams for a grown up who can serve as a back up when you can't make it to practice. Good character, discipline, loads of patience, and a sense of humor are qualifications as important as tennis skills.

Instead of one-on-one practice, you can hold group practice with kids from the same tennis class, supervised by a grown up. That way a group of parents can share supervision. Remember, the goal of practice is to repeat and reinforce what has been taught in class, so even a parent with reasonable skills is fine.

Finding a Junior Partner

As a child develops rally consistency emphasize more one-on-one practice sessions. She can now begin to be partnered with juniors at various skill levels. Against a more competent player the junior can develop rally consistency and learn to play under pressure.

Practicing with a player at the same skill level will help to cut down unforced errors. As both players are of equal ability, whoever makes fewer mistakes wins. Match-play practice with a player at a lower skill level will allow a child to learn to take chances and try shots recently learned. Always reward the effort of both players.

One way to find junior partners of various skill levels is from the classes taught by Pros. Usually a Pro runs classes for multiple levels, starting with the beginners – Peewees, Hotshots, Inter-club, and Challenger. Consider kids in the class one level higher and one level lower, as well as kids at the same skill level.

Schools, tennis clubs, community associations, and churches are good places to find juniors looking for practice partners. The number of tennis playing years may be an indicator of skill level, but a better way is to use the self-rating system called Junior National Tennis Rating Program (JNTRP). Contact your USTA section office for information about the JNTRP (More info: usta.com).

Team Practice

The USTA has developed programs to encourage kids to learn and practice as a team. If team practice is your child's thing, check out their USA Team Tennis (Youth) program (More info: usta.com). The program allows a junior to join a team in the area that matches his age and skill level. These teams then compete with other teams from the same geographic region.

Backboard Practice

Monica Seles found her tennis groove hitting against a wall in a parking lot with her dad and coach, Karolj. Judging from her famous grunt, she must have knocked quite a few holes in the wall. A wall or a tennis backboard can be a great hitting partner – it returns the ball every time.

However, experts caution against using a backboard to practice a stroke that is still shaky. Repeating an imperfect technique against a backboard will only make it harder to improve. Learn the stroke from a competent pro first. Used correctly, hitting the newly learned stroke against a backboard can teach consistency, placement, and concentration.

Right Way

Hitting a ball too hard against a backboard can make it come back much quicker than any real opponent. The danger is that the ball will contact the racket too late, developing a rushed, unnatural stroke. Here are some tips to help practice correctly:

✓ Use a nearly dead ball.
✓ When practicing groundstrokes, take the ball on the second bounce instead of the first.
✓ Give extra time for groundstrokes by standing about three feet more than the distance from the net to the baseline, approximately 14 grown-up steps.
✓ Contact the ball in front of the body.
✓ Use a removable tape to mark a net-line on the wall, three feet off the ground.
✓ Tape up bright-colored Court Donuts or Spots made of rubber to practice hitting groundstrokes above the net and for placing the serve. Better yet, bring along a Target Trainer and lean it against the backboard in a position you want to target-practice.

And, as always, remember to practice with a plan.

Drills and Games

Hitting against a wall doesn't have to be monotonous. There are literally dozens and dozens of backboard drills and games for solo practice. You can simulate play against another person and can even compete with the wall. For example, "Backboard Drills for Individuals and Groups" by Mike Bachicha and Dennis Van der Meer (More info: ptrtennis.org) provides instructors with 55 different backboards drills. In addition, the USTA has produced a video called "Backboard Tennis" that is available in tennis shops. The video illustrates plans perfect for solo practices.

Ball Machine Practice

So your junior has perfected a backhand slice. There are three ways to groove in the stroke using a ball machine – practice, practice, and more practice. Mike Agassi understood this when he set up a battery of ball machines at his backyard court, and son Andre hit the bumps, ball after ball.

It's important to learn the right stroke technique from a pro first. Otherwise, the player will end up reinforcing a bad stroke hundreds of times. Pick a specific stroke for the practice session, say the backhand slice, and use it against a majority of the balls.

We know ball machines can be relentless practice partners, tossing balls at preset speeds, spins, heights, depths, and directions. Ball machine practice will undoubtedly burn up calories, but that is not its main purpose, so practice to a stroke plan.

The machines on the market today can be programmed to toss a sequence of strokes of any type in any order – flat, lob, topspin, and slice. The machine can also place each ball to different specified locations on the court, making it possible to simulate match play conditions. Practice an approach shot by programming the machine to toss balls in patterns of two – first a short one to which the player hits deep; next sprint forward to receive a net ball and finish it off with a volley.

Maybe someday, the ball machine will learn advanced match play. After retaliating against a deep approach shot with a crosscourt passing shot, low with topspin and forcing you to return a weak volley, the machine rips the next ball as a passing shot down the line. Until then, be nice to your human practice partners and use the machine to groove in strokes and basic match play.

Easing into Competition

Fun is the name of the game for children under 10 years or so. After that children may begin to show interest in competing. Children have to be at least 13 to 14 years of age to have the maturity needed for serious competition with peers. In the interim, if the child continues to show enthusiasm for tennis, it is appropriate to transition from fun and games to light competition.

Learning about Competition

It does not matter whether a parent or coach had the opportunity to discuss the meaning and nature of competition with the child. Children learn about winning, losing, and competition from many others sources – television shows, for example. And remember the time when the tennis class was challenged to a game of King of the Court or bouncing the ball off the racket? Even though the emphasis is on fun and games, children quickly begin to pick up on the competitive nature of sport. As long as there is less emphasis on winning and losing, children begin to thrive on competition.

The more time a grown-up spends with a child on the court playing games and match play, the easier it will be for the child to transition from drills and games to competing with peers. They should learn that it's okay to lose and okay to win. A child can also understand this from watching tournaments on television. Pete Sampras might have lost in the first round of an ATP event, but within months he made a huge comeback to win the US Open.

First Competition

No format is better than the parent-child format to ease a kid into formal competition. Parent and child form a doubles team and compete with other parent-child pairs.

The parent-child format is like striking two birds with one tennis ball. The child earns his first participation wings under the emotional safety of a parent-partner. On the other hand, the parent gains an appreciation for the rigors of future competition. Above all, it is a format that is full of fun for both children and parents, even those who have never before played tennis.

Team Tennis is another great way to get your child started in competition. The USA Team Tennis (Youth) program offers recreational play and opportunities to learn in a group environment for kids ages 6 to 18. Unlike sanctioned tournaments that are regulated by the USTA, the USA Team Tennis (Youth) program is initiated at the local level by a professional coach from the area, a parent, a private club, the parks and recreation department, or a community tennis association (More info: usta.com). Match play is informal with friends and neighbors playing together.

4

Fun to Fiery

"Float like a butterfly, sting like a bee."
MUHAMMAD ALI, professional boxer.

Winning is not everything, but winning is important. To keep this in perspective, remember that enjoyment of the game comes first, and then everything else, including winning.

A peewee class is structured around fun and games. For little Johnny simply attending the class is fun. After a few years of tennis lessons, he gets in the groove, becomes more proficient. At this age the opportunity to participate and hang out with friends is a sufficient incentive. Approaching the adolescent years, Johnny develops additional motivators – competition and the desire to win.

The natural desire to compete and win ought to be accepted. A kid who wins more matches than he loses is likely to want to continue to play and improve his game. Acceptance of the natural desire to win, as opposed to emphasizing and pushing for a win, is in line with Sports psychologists who advise parents to de-emphasize wins and losses.

Learning to Win

"Learning to win starts off the court, with learning to learn," Coach Nick Bollettieri told Tennis magazine as he began coaching the professional from Chile, Marcelo Rios.

Winning not only requires giving your all during the match, more importantly, it means giving maximum effort preparing for the match. Start by becoming aware of your current strengths and weaknesses. Shut out unnecessary objectives and practice focusing on a few critical ones: overcoming a weak stroke, improving a specific strategy, and achieving peak physical condition in time for the competition.

Raising the Bar

At age 11, Tenille Elias had thrashed all comers and was ranked No. 1 among girls 16 and under on the family's native island of Trinidad.

She was running out of serious opponents there, so her dad entered Tenille in a tournament in Mexico.

Father and daughter were in for a shock. In a field of girls from the host country and around the Caribbean, Tenille hardly shined. In fact, she was dispatched in the second round. Hoping to raise the level of her game by seeking stiffer competition, Dad moved Tenille to a tennis academy in Florida.

When the probability of winning is very high, a player's record may seem impressive but the accomplishment is clearly devalued. Tennis development is sacrificed at the altar of easy wins. Often a kid loses motivation to improve and sometimes even to play.

Experts suggest a 2-to-1 win-loss record is about right to keep a kid motivated to play and, at the same time, continue to improve. When a kid is consistently winning two matches for every loss, it's time to raise the bar. Consider entering a few tournaments in a higher age group; practice and play with grown ups; or, if possible, move to a state or region where competition is more intense.

Becoming Assertive on Court

The Merriam-Webster dictionary defines assertion as "the act to state or declare positively and often forcefully or aggressively." A player might be the nicest person in the world off-court and display excellent sportsmanship on court. To win matches, though, the player has to show assertiveness in his game. Being too careful or making tentative shots in a match may indicate the need for a talk with the coach about a more aggressive game.

There are many programs available at local community centers that offer assertiveness training for kids. Practicing martial arts is a great way to develop assertiveness. If little Johnny does not improve his tennis as a result, at least he will succeed in gaining new respect from the school bully.

Broadening the Definition of Winning

By definition, there is only one winner in a tennis tournament – the winning finalist. If competition is to be beneficial to kids, they have to be taught to broaden their definition of winning and success.

A kid who practices his down-the-line passing shot and uses it effectively to win a third-round match is a success. A junior who reaches the semi-finals for the first time is a winner. That's not to say the junior should stop striving. In fact, he should enter the competition preparing to win the tournament. However, if the junior loses in the final round, after winning the first three rounds of a 16-player draw, he is a winner three times over and must be encouraged to believe that.

"Children should be encouraged to compete against their own potential," says Dr Alan Goldberg, a renowned sports psychologist. "Boys should focus on beating Mr. Peter Potential, competing against themselves, while the girls challenge Ms. Patty Potential."

Winners are also those who handle failure better. There is a widespread belief that great players were successful throughout their careers. Actually, champions probably just coped with their setbacks and losses better than their opponents did. Andre Agassi fell from single to triple digits in the rankings between 1996 and 1997 while he put on weight and dealt with personal problems.

Then his coach, Brad Gilbert, initiated the well-known reclamation project. Gilbert convinced Agassi to work his way back into form – mentally and physically – by entering a few Challenger tournaments, which are professional tennis' minor leagues. The story of how Agassi, the once-showy superstar, had to get his own towels and flip his own scoreboard without complaining is now the stuff of legend. It is also folklore how Agassi has since regained his top ranking, winning many more Grand Slams and professional titles.

I Don't Want To Win

We want to believe winning makes a tennis kid happy and that losing makes him sad. Peel away the superficial emotions and you may be surprised to learn that your kid sometimes feels conflicted after a win - happy, anxious, and even guilty. Conversely, after a loss he may actually feel secretly happy and relieved.

Timothy Gallwey, author of best-selling book Inner Game of Tennis, ascribes possible reasons why a player could become conflicted about winning. The challenge for parents and coaches is that these reactions to winning are natural for most kids:

- If I win and become the champion, I'll have to remain champion or disappoint myself and be criticized for not living up to expectations.
- If I beat my friend Harry, he'll be angry with me.
- If I win too much, I won't be able to keep my friendship with fellow players.
- I won't put in my maximum effort. That way I will have an excuse if I lose.

De-emphasizing wins and losses, especially during the early years, is a first step toward combating these attitudes. Encourage giving maximum effort and always celebrate the effort, whether the child wins or loses.

Find a quiet time away from the bustle of immediate competition and talk to your child about these pre- and post-match emotions. For example, while you chaperone the kid to and from lessons tell him what you know about fear of losing and fear of winning. Help the child understand that these are natural reactions.

Explain how he can overcome these negative attitudes by focusing on each point, rather than on the ultimate result of the match. Let the child know that giving maximum effort is your only expectation of him and that you will celebrate his effort regardless of the outcome.

Playing a Friend

In local competition kids invariably have to compete against friends, which can be hard on them. Timothy Gallwey describes the nature of competition using a simple but enlightening example that even a 10-year old can understand and tuck away in his subconscious.

Imagine the right and left hands to represent opposing players. Center the hands between your knees. Competing means the right hand aims to push the left hand past the left knee and vice versa. After pushing each other, say the right hand wins. Do you applaud the right hand and view it with respect and show disdain for the left hand? Of course not, you will simply accept the result. Also, say you do this five minutes each day making sure each hand puts in maximum effort in the competition. Ultimately, both hands will become stronger, no matter how many wins and losses each hand has.

Help your child understand that giving maximum effort in a match is a way to better himself as well as the other player. He will be less anxious about competing against friends. After all, "compete" comes from the Latin word "competere," meaning to seek together.

The Next Coach

A few years of fun and games have gone by and now your child is entering the development phase. In the beginner phase a coach's primary focus is to get the child interested in tennis and teach the basics. While the game should never cease to be fun, the next stage –

the development phase – requires new roles and offers fresh challenges for a coach.

Development Phase

The development phase will generally start during the kid's pre-adolescent years. In this phase the coach should be able to impart a higher level of skill and demand discipline. Working with kids through their teen years poses a unique set of challenges. Unless the coach has a successful track record teaching kids at both the beginner and development levels, you may want to transition from your child's first coach to the next.

In choosing a coach for the development phase, first satisfy yourself that the basics have been met: an appropriate certification and ability to make practice enjoyable. New considerations for the selection process are:

- Commitment: Look for a coach who teaches tennis full-time. Coaching at this level demands greater commitment. Being available for a special pre-competition workout may be important. An adolescent may need emotional attention, outside of tennis practice, to prepare him mentally for competition.
- Emphasis on mastery: The best coaches focus on making a player simply better, rather than making the player better than a certain opponent. All-around development – psychological, physical, tactical, and technical – is more important than a good-looking record full of easy wins that will later crumble in the face of higher-level competition. The ability to guide kids toward performance goals is extremely valuable. For example, achieving a 60 percent consistency in first-serves is more important than chasing ranking points.

High-Performance Phase

This phase represents the advanced regional and national levels of junior competition. By now the on-court role of the parent may have diminished considerably. It is likely the junior will be spending more hours than ever with the coach each day in practice, workouts, and tournament travel.

Finding a Nick Bollettieri, Robert Lansdorp, Nick Saviano, or Paul Annacone won't hurt. You want a coach with a respectable track record at this level and the time to offer personal training. Be unabashed in asking about his successful protégés at this level of competition.

Coaching kids, especially teenagers, is a challenge to say the least. Sometimes coaches burnout, too. Current continuing education credits and recent protégés who have reached the top at regional and national levels indicate the coach is motivated and excited. Your child will be, too.

From One Coach to the Next

Tennis development aside, a parent may have to find a new coach because of relocation, scheduling issues and so on. Whatever the reason, try to make the switch from one coach to the next amicable and gradual.

The toughest transition for a kid would be from the fun and games of the beginner phase, lasting two to four years, to the more technical and demanding development phase. Ideally, let the kid continue attending classes with the first coach and start private lessons with the next. Add group lessons with the new coach, followed by match play, and finally move to a full schedule.

The transition could occur over a year or more. For some the transition is never truly complete. Chris Evert's dad was always her primary coach. Over the years she chose several coaches that complemented her primary coach. Each brought something different and useful to the player-coach relationship.

Breaking the Mold

In the late 1960s, Dick Fosbury, a high schooler from Oregon and an avid high jumper, shattered the Olympic record, clearing 7 feet 4-1/2 inches. More significant than winning the Olympic gold medal was the way in which Fosbury won this event.

For decades, virtually all high jumpers were coached to use a method called the straddle. The jumper kicks one foot up and rolls over the bar with the face down. The straddle method depended on leg strength. Dick Fosbury was taught to use the straddle method when he started high jumping. But his jumps were mediocre at best. He began experimenting with a scissors method, popularized by children leaping fences.

Eventually, he refined this technique and actually started to jump up and over backwards, knee, chest, and face to the sky. The technique needed less leg strength, produced higher jumps, and was so revolutionary it got its own name: the Fosbury Flop. The Flop earned Dick Fosbury the Olympic gold.

Tennis is no different. Some of the game's greatest improvements came about because a coach or player chose to break the mold and experiment with unorthodox techniques. Of course, advances in rackets, shoes, and surfaces make them practical.

Andre Agassi's open stance, short backswing, and shoulder turn on the return-of-serve were quite unheard of in his junior days. The single-handed backhand that Pete Sampras' coach encouraged him to use may have taken a year or so to perfect. But look what a success that experiment has been for Sampras! Running around the backhand to hit a forehand was unheard of until Steffi Graf wielded this unorthodox technique like a weapon.

Bedrock fundamentals won't change: good balance, contacting in front, shoulder movement, and so on. Still, there is tremendous room for innovation in technique and tactics. Go forth and experiment.

O'Connell's Ball Control Contest

"You can't manage what you can't measure." The point of this famous quote by management guru, Peter Drucker, is that effective management requires feedback, knowing that you are progressing toward your objectives. Regular measurement is key to continuous improvement.

Measuring Stroke Ability

Drucker's theory is applicable to managing anything that has investments in time, money, and effort, including junior tennis development. Win-loss records and junior rankings are some ways to measure a junior's progress. However, just as in the beginner phase, experts advise against over-emphasizing wins-losses and rankings during the tennis development phase.

When competition rankings and points are used as the sole measure of progress an unreasonable burden is placed on the coach and the junior. Easy wins will be emphasized over tennis development. We know this is true because many youngsters with sterling rankings in the 12s and 14s seem to suddenly hit a brick wall at the higher echelons of competition. Junior competition is an essential part of tennis development, but by measuring stroke ability you encourage the development of solid fundamentals and an all-round game.

The Contest

Dan O'Connell, a USPTA professional, presents a method he calls the 200-point Ball Control Contest. The method is a quick and fun way to measure progress without the risk of placing too much emphasis on junior rankings during the early development years. This method is also a great tool for helping a coach decide into which level a new student fits. A parent or coach can use the 200-point contest to determine when a kid is ready to move from the development to the high-performance phase.

Testing takes about two hours and requires a hitting wall, a stopwatch, and two flat 48-foot ropes. There are 200 total points to be earned: 100 points in two groundstroke tests and 100 more in tests on overhead, volley, and serve.

O'Connell has validated the contest by his test results, proving that the higher the score, the better the player's technique and stroke ability.

Groundstroke Depth Game

This tests consistency of groundstrokes targeted deep toward the baseline. Two ropes are laid to create 6-foot sections between the baseline and service line on one side of the court.

Twenty balls are fed from the service line so that they land behind the opposite service line. Balls are fed without a pattern, using a variety of heights, depths, and directions – about 10 forehand shots and 10 backhand shots.

The scorer will record the result of each shot on a scoring sheet. There are seven scoring marks. Balls that are hit into the net are marked N. Balls hit into the service box are marked S for short. Wide balls are marked W and long balls are marked L. Points can only be scored when a ball lands in the 6-foot sections of the backcourt marked by the ropes. Balls landing in the shallow section receive one point, those that land in the middle score two points, and balls landing in the deepest area score three points.

Passing Shot Game

This tests proficiency in groundstroke passing shots. Two ropes are placed six feet inside each singles sideline, parallel to the lines. Each shot landing in this area gains a point.

The Passing Shot game is four tests of 10 balls: (1) forehand down the line, (2) forehand crosscourt, (3) backhand down the line, (4) backhand crosscourt. Balls are fed with a pattern, so they land in a similar area behind the service line.

On the forehand tests, the balls are fed off-center to the forehand side, and on the backhand tests the balls are fed off-center to the backhand side. After the student hits each ball, he shuffle-steps back to the center service mark before moving quickly to hit the next shot.

Service Game

Place a rope six feet inside the service line. Ten balls are served into the deuce court and ten into the advantage court. All serves that land in the deepest area of the service court marked by the rope score two points, and all other balls that land in the short area of the service box earn one point. A total of 40 points can be earned.

Volley Game

The player is positioned six feet from the wall and hits as many alternating forehand-backhand volleys as possible in 20 seconds. One point is earned for each volley hit against the wall. Balls must clear net height.

Overhead Game

Place a rope six feet behind the service line. Feed 10 balls suitable to hit overhead shots.

Two points are earned for each ball that lands in the deeper area of the court as marked by the rope. One point is earned for balls landing in the short area of the court. No points are earned for balls hit out of the court.

Point Tally

Total up the results from the four games to determine standings in stroke-proficiency (Table 4.1):

Table 4.1

	Champion	Tournament Player	Advanced Player	Challenger	Future Star
Groundstroke Depth Game	40 or more	33-39	25-32	20-24	19 or less
Passing Shot Game	36 or more	32-35	27-31	21-26	20 or less
Service Game	32 or more	28-31	24-27	20-23	19 or less
Volley Game	40 or more	35-39	30-34	20-29	19 or less
Overhead Game	16 or more	14-15	12-13	10-11	9 or less
	150 or more	135-149	120-134	100-119	99 or less

The results also help identify a player's strengths and areas where more work is needed.

5

Competition

"I've always had those little goals that I've worked toward – they add up."
STACY ALLISON, first American woman to climb Mt. Everest.
BeyondtheLimits.com.

Why does Johnny hate sports? There may be many reasons, but competition is definitely not one of them. One of the big myths is that children hate sports because of competition. Just ask any child who is good in a particular sport if he would like to compete and the answer is invariably a resounding, "Yes!"

The reason competition gets a bad rap is because children are thrust into tournaments before they can become reasonably good for that level of play. A child will enjoy competing at every level – rookie to elite – provided he develops sufficient proficiency to sustain a good balance of wins and losses. Experts suggest that, in tennis, two or three wins for every loss is a ratio that will motivate a young child to continue wanting to improve and compete.

Is Junior Ready?

Most parents and coaches don't want to hurt or pressure their kids and risk burn out. However, in every sport there comes a time when the junior necessarily has to compete against an opponent, either a person or the scoreboard, as in golf. It is the fundamental nature of sport that one must beat the opponent or lose.

Losing hurts, and though winning feels good, some children become anxious when they win in an early round because it means they have to face a tough opponent in the next round – fear of winning. The thinking process goes something like this: "If I win against this guy, I'll have to win against him every time or disappoint myself and be criticized for not living up to expectations." That's why players with better ability sometimes lose to less competent opponents. So the question is, when is a child mature enough to handle wins and losses without too much anxiety?

The other issue to think about is the child's level of competency in the sport. Consider a crossover scenario in which a 14-

year-old soccer player switches to tennis. She has been playing competitive soccer for several years and may be mentally mature enough to handle wins and losses.

Should the young lady take a few tennis lessons and jump straight into competition? Most people would say probably not, because, although mentally prepared for competition, she is clearly not ready from the perspective of technical ability. Clearly, both technical competency and mental maturity must come into play when deciding if junior is ready for competition.

Technical Competency

As parents we are unabashedly biased when it comes to judging the technical ability of our kids. After all, little Jill is the best tennis player in her age group, right? Even though the world may think otherwise. Judging technical readiness for competition is best left to an experienced coach.

Brent Zeller, a tennis teacher since 1974 and founder of Effortless Tennis – a system that teaches skill development before competition – has developed an empirical assessment plan that tests whether a junior has achieved the minimum level of technical competency necessary for competition. His plan, called Effortless Challenge also demands a basic level of mental and emotional maturity.

The one-hour assessment plan to judge readiness for playing competitive tennis is a series of stroke consistency exercises (Table 5.1). These are cooperative exercises, so there should be no hitting winners. Form counts, no hacking. If a player misses a shot, or hits a shot different from the one she is supposed to hit, start over.

It may be best to take the assessment readings without fanfare and as a part of junior's regular class schedule. We don't want to get into a pass/fail scenario. When a player successfully completes all these exercises, Zeller suggests they have developed a sound foundation for competitive play.

Mental Maturity

America's Funniest Home Videos televised an episode in which a 3-year-old, frustrated with a computer challenge game, sobs and screams at the monitor, "I want to win! I want to win!"

Psychologists say children 8 years old and under are not mentally mature enough to handle the rigors of competition. Between

Table 5.1

Zeller's Effortless Challenge		
Type of Stroke	**Exercise**	**Minimum shots in a row per person**
Ground-stroke	**1.** Short court groundstroke rally	20
	Both players stand three feet behind service line and hit so ball lands inside service line. Mix strokes up between forehand and backhand.	
	2. Baseline groundstroke rally	15
	Players gravitate to the middle of the court after each shot.	
	3. Crosscourt groundstroke rallies	10
	Players first complete a forehand rally and then backhand rally. Player gravitates to the middle of the court after each shot.	
	4. Down the line groundstroke rallies	10
	Player first completes a forehand rally and then backhand rally. Player gravitates to the middle of the court after each shot.	
Volley	**5.** Short court volley-groundstroke rally	20
	Volleying player stands three to four feet from the net. Other player stands three feet behind service line. Volleys must land inside service line. Mix strokes up between forehand and backhand.	
	6. Baseline volley-groundstroke rally	15
	Volleying player stands near the net. Mix strokes up between forehand and backhand.	
	7. Volley-volley rally	10
	Players stand three feet inside the service line. Players first complete a forehand rally and then backhand rally.	
Serve	**8.** Serve	10
	Ball must clear baseline before second bounce. Players first serve into the ad side and then deuce side.	
Return of Serve	**9.** Return of Serve	10
	Ball must clear baseline before second bounce. Return from each side of the court.	
Lob and Overhead	**10**. Lob-overhead rally	10
	The net player hits overheads and the baseline player lobs.	

8 and 10 years of age children can be eased into competition with parent-child tournaments and team tennis. This is also the time when children need to be taught about handling wins and losses. Some kids develop the maturity necessary to want to enter and win competitions after age 10. More commonly, this happens at age 12 or 13.

Until then, they should be taking lessons and practicing match play. Having successfully completed the technical competency exercises, the young lady can't wait to enter the local tournament. It's time for her to enjoy the ride.

Having the mental maturity to face competition is less of an issue for older kids that crossover from other sports. The Gullickson twins, Tim and Tom, were all-state high-school basketball players. They didn't play much tennis in their junior years and didn't compete in a single national junior tournament.

The Gullicksons entered their first serious tennis competition at Northern Illinois University and became one of the top professional doubles teams in the country, until their retirement in 1986. Tim went on to coach the world's No. 1, Pete Sampras.

Draws

The Draw. Sounds like a Clint Eastwood classic, doesn't it? A junior single-elimination draw can be just as exciting. The tournament draw determines who gets to play whom. The draw sheet published online and displayed at the tournament site may also indicate the place and time of matches. The single-elimination is the most common kind of tournament draw. If a player loses, he is out; if he wins, he goes on to the next round.

So your junior has honed his technique, practiced match play, and is now entering his first tournament. You pay the $25 registration fee, put life on hold for a day and drive 60 miles to the tournament site. In 30 minutes, junior has lost his first match and is out of the competition.

A first-round loss in a singles-elimination draw can be heartbreaking for a rookie junior and frustrating for the parent. That's why tournaments open to rookies offer draw formats that give juniors a chance to play a few matches, even after losing.

The consolation format guarantees a player at least two matches. If a player loses an early round match, they are placed into a consolation bracket, where they continue to play until they lose. Better yet, consolation matches often count toward regional rankings.

The compass is a player-friendly format that guarantees players multiple matches, even if they lose every match. For example, each player in a draw of 16 is guaranteed 4 matches. After the first round, winners go to the east draw and others to the west draw. Second round winners continue in the same direction, while others move to north and south draws respectively to form a new satellite tournament (More info: usta.com). For larger draw sizes things can get so confusing that everyone goes home happy, believing they won the tournament.

The best format to gain competition experience is the round robin, which is ideal for small draws of eight or so players. This format guarantees multiple matches for each player as they play against all others in their flight. This format is ideal for parent-child, small club, and rookie tournaments.

Junior Ranking

Put together a bunch of computers, a team of computer savvy folks, loads of experience and smarts from the USTA, and you've got the Junior Ranking system.

For parents who feel a computerized ranking system is sometimes unfair, consider the alternative. A mountain of avoidable paperwork for players, tournament directors, and the USTA. Ranking and selection committees would inevitably be accused of playing politics and power mongering because the ranking computation depends on so many complex variables. And then there are the protest committees who must give a hearing to players and parents who believe they got the short end of the stick.

The computerized ranking system is far from perfect but at least no one can accuse it of bias against a specific player. More work can be done to make administration easier and bring tournaments online.

Ranking Defined

A player's ranking is a number that reflects the quality of his match results compared to other competitors over a specified period of time, usually January through December. Tournaments that count toward the ranking are sanctioned by the USTA at the district, section, or national levels.

Ranking is not intended to measure a player's skill level. Neither is it a guaranteed indicator of future performance. If that were the case, a junior ranked No. 1 would become No. 1 in the professional rankings, which is not necessarily true. Consider ranking as simply an assessment of a player's past match record.

Ranking System

Rankings are based on a Points-per-round ranking system that awards ranking points based on the round a player reaches in a tournament. In some systems, bonus points are also awarded for wins over top players. "Round Points" based on how far a player advances in a tournament and "Quality Points" based on quality of opponent.

Lists

Fortunately, there is plenty of room at the top of the ranking mountain. There are a variety of ranking lists at the national, sectional, and district levels for every age group. At the national level you have Singles Ranking, Doubles Ranking, National Selection and Seeding, Super National Selection, National Open Qualifiers, and Wild Card Lists (More info: usta.com). Sectional and district lists are based on match results in regional as well as national tournaments held in the region.

Each list has different uses. For instance, the National Selection and Seeding list assists tournament directors in selecting players into limited draw events and in seeding for events. The Super National Selection list, as its name implies, is used to select a limited number of players directly into Super National Championships.

Perks

Obviously, there is no guarantee that a No. 1 ranked junior will win the next tournament he enters, but earning a high ranking sure has its perks:

✓ Entries to tournaments: If the number of entrants exceeds the draw limit, a Tournament Committee may bump out the lower ranked players. Many high-profile tournaments are restricted to a qualified number of ranked players. Sectional and district level top rankers usually receive endorsements to participate at the nationals.

✓ Better draw placements: A highly ranked player may earn seeding in a tournament. This means he or she won't be confronting other highly ranked players in the early rounds. Like a self-fulfilling prophecy, this gives the player a better chance of winning the tournament, which in turn further improves his ranking.

✓ Special opportunities: Top players have the opportunity to attend competition training camps and become eligible for regional and national team events like the Junior Davis Cup.

✓ Financial benefits: Colleges consider a player's rank when awarding athletic scholarships. Grants may be offered to a top ranked player to cover travel and other expenses. A player who wishes to turn professional should know that a good ranking and solid recent performance are important factors sponsors consider.

✓ Goal setting: Rankings provide short- and long-term goals for the young competitor. Consistent improvement in ranking means player, coach, and parent are all doing something right. If a junior's ranking is uneven or going downhill, it's time to go back to the drawing board.

Of course being No. 1, even for a while, bestows never-ending campus bragging rights, too.

Points-based Ranking System: The Inside Skinny

Understanding how junior rankings are computed can help parents and players pick which and how many tournaments to play to earn a good ranking. So put on your arithmetic cap and hop along on the junior circuit.

Round Points

In the Points-based Ranking System (PRS), a player earns round-points as he advances in the tournament. The amount of points that can be earned depends upon the strength of the tournament field.

For example, the USTA Florida section awards just two points for advancing to the quarterfinals of a Rookie tournament. Reaching the same round in a Super Series can earn a player up to 31 points (More info: usatennisflorida.usta.com). Similarly, at the national level the USTA has developed a Ranking Point Table that specifies the points for each round and level of tournament (More info: usta.com).

Bonus Points

In singles competition, bonus points are awarded for having wins over "top 100" ranked player. The Ranking Points earned at the tournament is therefore round points plus bonus points.

Ranking Value

The national system and many USTA sections consider a player's best 8 tournaments in the last 12 months when determining the rankings. Ranking Value is simply the total number of ranking points earned at the player's best 8 tournaments.

Rank

To the player with the highest-ranking value goes the honor – rank No. 1 and so on. Although it's tempting to enter high-level tournaments with larger round points, professionals recommend playing the level best suited to develop competitive skills. It is advantageous to compete in as many tournaments as practical so the best results will be taken into account.

This is all probably more than you ever wanted to know about the ranking system, but an overview like this is necessary to understand how it all works. Feel free to take off the arithmetic cap now; you looked weird wearing it anyway.

The basic concept of the PRS system is straightforward, but you have hundreds of ranking lists of various age groups, formats, and levels. There are also thousands of players and matches and more than a few quirks – defaults, walkovers, and matches against non-ranked players. Now you see why you need lots of computers, a team of computer savvy folks, and smarts from the USTA.

Earning a Ranking

Recreational play, long-term skill development, and mental maturity are important reasons why younger age groups are not encouraged to compete for rankings. Younger children can gain tournament experience by playing in novice tournaments that don't count toward rankings. Once a kid develops a level of competitive maturity, the rankings race can be an exciting goal for the junior.

To earn a ranking, players must accumulate a specified number of participation points by competing in sanctioned tournaments in their age category. Usually three to seven tournaments are needed to be eligible for district or sectional ranking. In addition, a player must earn a specified number of ranking points in the 12 month period, generally 200 points before a ranking can be assigned.

After racking up the participation and ranking points, presto! Junior's name is up in rankings list. You can access the rankings list and your player record on the USTA website (More info: usta.com) or on the sectional and district websites. It's important to verify player records and report any inaccuracies.

Welcome to the race! To improve ranking, enter tournaments that offer a good chance of winning against slightly stronger opponents. Play as many tournaments as possible but don't burn out. Keep it simple, don't over-manage ranking. Enjoy the learning experience. Have fun!

Rating

While ranking is earned by playing sanctioned tournaments, many of which are based on age divisions, rating is simply a visual determination of skill level, irrespective of age.

The USA Team Tennis (Youth) program uses the Junior National Tennis Rating Program (JNTRP) guidelines to match boys and girls in a certain age group to play on teams of similar ability (Table 5.2).

For example, a 12-year-old just starting tennis with a JNTRP of 1.0 would be placed in a beginner league called 12s Red division. Another kid of the same age but with a JNTRP of 3.0 would be assigned the 12s White division so she can play matches compatible with her advanced skill level. A coach, trained parent, or player can perform the visual rating.

Goal Setting

Ten-year old Mary says her goal is to keep improving her game, whereas her classmate Joanne's dream is to win the US Open. Provided they practice well and develop and accomplish short-term goals regularly there is a chance Mary will continue to accomplish her goal and Joanne might one day adorn the finals at Arthur Ashe Stadium. There is a critical difference, though, between Mary's goal and Joanne's dream.

Process Goal vs. Outcome Goal

Mary has committed to performance-oriented improvement relative to her own capabilities. If Mary practices smarter and harder it is likely she will get better. Mary has good control of the potential and successful outcome of her goal.

By age 16, Mary's continuous improvement earns her a sponsorship deal that allows her to receive high performance training. As her focus is still on improving her game, she gets so good that in a

Table 5.2

Junior National Tennis Rating Program	
	General Characteristics of Various Playing Levels
1.0	Player is just starting to play tennis and is learning the basic skills of serving, forehands, backhands, and volleys.
1.5	Player is only slightly more advanced than a 1.0 player. Player needs to coordinate moving when hitting the ball. In fact, player is still concentrating on getting the ball over the net from a stationary position. Player is learning to serve and keep score.
2.0	Player is now beginning to coordinate footwork when contacting the ball but is not consistent in hitting the ball over the net. Player can serve to some degree but double faults frequently. Player understands scoring as well as correct positions for serving and receiving. Player has limited success with volley but has knowledge of court positioning in both singles and doubles.
2.5	Player is able to judge where the ball is going. Player can sustain a slow-paced rally of several shots with someone of the same ability, using both forehand and backhand sides, and can volley with moderate success. Player can keep score unassisted, call own lines, serve overhand from the baseline and has an understanding of the basic rules.
3.0	Player is getting better at moving to the ball and is improving court coverage; can sustain a rally with consistency on slow to moderate-paced shots. Player serves with fair consistency with few double faults. On groundstrokes, player needs to improve control of height, depth, direction, and speed. Player attempts to move opponent from side to side and hit to the opponent's weakness.
3.5	Player can sustain a rally and is beginning to develop directional control and depth of groundstrokes. Player is starting to recognize opportunities to attack short balls by coming to the net. Player is developing more spin and power on the serve and seldom double faults. Player is becoming more aggressive and applying basic strategy in singles and using teamwork in doubles.
4.0	Player has dependable strokes, including directional control and depth on higher-paced shots and has good court coverage. Player has added variety in shot selection by using lobs, overheads, volleys, and approach shots with some success. Player is developing a game plan, is serving with good consistency, and is now forcing some errors with power and/or spin. Player demonstrates good teamwork in doubles.

Table 5.2 *(continued from previous page)*

Junior National Tennis Rating Program	
	General Characteristics of Various Playing Levels
4.5	Player has a very dependable game and executes most shots consistently on higher-paced shots. Player's court coverage and footwork are sound and player has begun to muster the use of power and spins. Player can vary depth of shots and game plan according to opponents. Player's first serve may produce some winners and second serves are hit with good spin and placement. Player can be aggressive in both singles and doubles and covers weaknesses well. Player is developing an offensive weapon.
5.0	Player has good shot anticipation and frequently has an outstanding shot or weapon around which a game can be structured. Player can regularly hit winners or force errors on short balls and is capable of all shots. Player's first serve is an offensive weapon and often allows rushing the net after the first or second serve. Volleys and overhead smashes are typically winning shots. Player is match-wise and uses shots that have a high percentage of success in both singles and doubles.

few years she is able to win a Grand Slam. She worked hard and was able to continually improve and accomplish her process or performance goal. This led her to a desirable outcome – winning a Grand Slam.

Obviously, winning a Grand Slam was not entirely accidental for Mary. She put that possibility in the back of her mind as one of the desirable outcomes of her hard work. Other outcomes she hoped for were to maintain a healthy weight, make the junior high and high school teams, achieve a top 10 sectional ranking, develop travel opportunities, earn a college scholarship, and sign a sponsorship deal.

Mary's goal was always centered on the process – improving her game. In the event that one or two desirable outcomes didn't pan out, Mary would still feel like a winner. Not because her friends and parents tell her so, but because, in her heart, she knows she is accomplishing her goal – improving her game – and, as a result, achieving many other desirable outcomes.

On the other hand, Joanne was just lucky she won a Grand Slam. Granted, Joanne worked very hard from early childhood and was focused on the dream of winning a Grand Slam. However, unlike Mary, who had a great deal of control over her goal, Joanne only "believed" she had full control of the outcome because she worked harder than anybody else she knew.

It is commendable that Joanne was strong and confident in her beliefs and she does deserve to win. In spite of that, we know Joanne had, at best, only partial control over the outcome, simply because there are too many other players who practiced just as hard as Joanne did and believed just as strongly that *they* would win a Grand Slam.

A long-term outcome goal like Joanne's has too many external factors that can undermine the result. For instance, moving to a new town might not allow sufficient court time; or there may be a lack of financial support due to changed circumstances; an unexpected injury might occur; or Joanne might face an opponent who is just too good on that match day.

Assume that, for whatever reason, Joanne is unable to win the Grand Slam, even though she won two other prestigious events leading up to the Slam. She might naturally feel like a failure because she was not able to fulfill her dream, something she had worked toward for many years.

Misconceptions about Process Goals

There are two common misconceptions about process goals. One is that they are less ambitious and thus encourage mediocrity. Not true. A player can be as ambitious as she wants in setting a process goal. The difference is that there is a high degree of correlation between a player's effort and the successful achievement of a process or performance goal.

For instance, Mary can choose to increase her first-serve percentage to 80 percent. This is ambitious for Mary, but if she is well coached and works hard, there is a high probability she can achieve the goal because, ultimately, it is up to her. When she does achieve her process goal, she may also experience a desirable outcome – winning the nationals.

The other misconception about process goals is that "improving the game" is not a clear or real goal. Ask yourself two questions: Is the goal measurable? Can the long-term goal be broken down into short-term goals? If your answer to one of these questions is, "yes," then the goal is clear, and it's real. In this case, "improving the game" can be measured – Mary improved her ranking. The goal can also be broken into many short-term goals: improving first-serve percentage to 80 percent, doing 10 extra push-ups in a conditioning routine, and so on.

"Having fun" is another completely valid process goal. At first it might not appear to be a goal at all, and even if it is, how can fun be measured? Tell that to the toy manufacturers. These guys know that when a kid picks up a toy his single-minded goal is to have fun. Toy manufacturers routinely use a scientific method called the Likert-type scale to measure fun when studying which of the many toy models has the best potential in the market. For our purposes, we could link "having fun" to a short-term goal such as, "I will engage in an activity I enjoy for three hours each week over the next month." We have just found a way to measure "having fun."

"Improving the game" and "having fun" are different from do-your-best goals such as, "Next year I will try to do the best I can." This goal can neither be measured directly nor can it be divided into measurable short-term goals.

Setting and measuring an outcome goal may be simple – "I want to win a Grand Slam when I grow up" – as compared to a process goal. However, experts recommend, and sports psychology literature clearly indicates, that process goals, when correctly and consistently utilized, allow a player to achieve greater success than either outcome or do-your-best goals.

Still, children are natural dreamers. A dream can be a great source of motivation to work hard. Encourage their dreams but help them understand the difference between a dream and a process goal. Children should be taught to chase process goals and enjoy each accomplishment. That is the practical way to make children feel successful, whether or not all dreams come true.

Finding a Tournament

It's great to be a tennis kid – nearly 5,500 tournament opportunities, thousands of team competitions to choose from, and a good parent or coach driving to and from competition sites. And when the vehicle is equipped with a rear-seat DVD entertainment system, life can't get any better for a tennis kid.

There are tournaments and leagues that cater to every skill level – rookie to advanced and all junior age groups under 10s-to-18s – with a variety of competition formats. The best place to start looking for tournaments is at your local tennis club. Chances are, the club runs tournaments and links with a junior competitive structure. Many clubs have teams that travel together.

Contact the tennis organizations involved in junior competition to find tournaments that match set criteria:

✓ USTA National, Sectional, and District offices for tournaments and USA Team Tennis programs in your area (More info: usta.com). USA Team Tennis programs revolve around three seasons: spring, summer, and fall.
✓ USPTA Junior Circuit (More info: uspta.com).
✓ Little Mo Tournament (More info: mcbtennis.org).
✓ World Team Tennis Junior Nationals (More info: worldteamtennis.com).
✓ High school tournaments are generally directed by a state-level interscholastic federation. For example, the California Interscholastic Federation (More info: cifstate.org) manages school tournaments in that state. Hook up with the school coach or your local school board to learn more.
✓ ITF Junior Circuit includes international tournaments from 14s to 18s. The circuit also includes team competitions – World Junior Tennis, Junior Davis Cup, and Junior Fed Cup (More info: itfjuniors.com). The circuit is a must to gain international competitive experience.

If you don't find an appropriate level and format in your area, consider organizing a tournament or team competition. Just make sure there are enough kids who want to compete and contact your local tennis organization. A little legwork, some financial savvy, and you can have a junior competition to call your own.

Picking the Right Tournament

After the coach and type of class, picking the right tournaments to enter determines whether a player is going to be self-motivated to practice and compete. First, make a list of performance or process goals for the year and write down all the desirable outcomes that are possible once each goal is accomplished.

Recreational Play

Brandon, a 14-year-old, moved with his family from upstate New York to Southern California. As there are no ice hockey rinks in the new town, he hopes to learn and play tennis, the sport that is popular there. Brandon's process goals are having fun and making friends. His desirable outcomes are recreation, fitness, and having friends to hang out with outside of school and sports.

For his age group and beginner level of play, Brandon would want to enter the Blue stars division of USA Team Tennis (Youth). This team tennis division is designed for beginners ages 13 to 18 that want to learn and play tennis for its recreational and social benefits. After a few seasons, if Brandon's win-loss ratio is at least 2:1, he could consider moving to the more advanced Blue stripes division.

Game Development

Consider the example of a junior who is seriously into competitive tennis. Ten-year-old Cathy has spent the last few years learning tennis with a professional coach. Along the way she competed in a few parent-child tournaments. Cathy can't wait to get into tournaments. Most USTA sections run Novice tournaments that are one-day events in which players face numerous opponents over the course of several hours.

If Cathy maintains a good win-loss ratio at a few Novice tournaments, she could advance to the Satellites and then to the Opens that count toward ranking. If Cathy is unable to maintain a positive win-loss ratio at Novice tournaments, she may not be ready for competition. A few more weeks of clinics and match play practice ought to do the trick.

Watching the early rounds of a tournament before actually entering one should give a good idea of the competition. At the Novice or Satellite levels, look for tournaments closer to home, preferably on courts the child is already familiar with. Draws that have consolation formats are nice. They give the child a chance to play several matches, even if she loses the first one.

Choice Table

Making a bottom-line choice is easy. If a junior simply wants to try tennis for a few seasons as one of many sports she would like to develop, then USA Team Tennis is the way to go. On the other hand, a junior who has made a choice to develop tennis as her primary sport and makes time throughout the year for practice and play will have access to hundreds of tournament opportunities.

With a variety of choices available in both team and tournament tennis, picking the right competition can be tricky. A sample format (Table 5.3) to help select the right program or tournament based on age group, current proficiency, and process goals can be useful.

The format is not nearly as complicated as it looks. Start by listing all possible tennis-related process goals. (Table 5.3 – Part 1). Later we will narrow it down to the goals junior wants to accomplish this year, but for now simply list all the possibilities. List the practice times and tournaments (or programs). Include various age groups and proficiency levels available at the local, regional, and national levels.

Third, list all possible tennis-related, near-term desirable outcomes (Table 5.3 – Part 2), continuing along the same row as the "process goals." Remember the difference: a process goal is one over which one has a fair degree of control. A desirable outcome is a possibility over which one has little control.

Now, for each competition, review the tournament regulations and checkmark all the possible process goals and desirable outcomes. For example, some of the best kids compete in the Southern California Tennis Association (SCTA) Designated tournaments. Participation in these tournaments can help a new player gain regional competitive experience and improve mental toughness; checkmark these two process goals for the SCTA Designated tournaments. In addition to accomplishing these process goals, a kid who does well in these tournaments can earn sectional endorsement to national tournaments – a desirable outcome; checkmark this desirable outcome for the SCTA Designated tournaments.

Using the Choice Table is the easy part. For her age group and current proficiency, the junior has to find the best match in the table for the process goals she intends to accomplish this year. This will point the junior to the right set of tournaments and programs and indicate how many hours of practice and match play are needed to accomplish those goals.

Measure progress at the end of the year. Junior is a happy camper if most process goals have been accomplished and one or two of the desirable outcomes have occurred. If not, consider adjusting process goals and practice time the following year.

Updating the Choice Table at the beginning of each year is a great way to get a tennis kid started on developing new process goals for the year. It also is a great help in allocating practice and playtime, and in choosing competitions that can help her accomplish those goals.

Table 5.3

Choice Table – Part 1 of 2
Sample Format to Pick the Right Tournament Based Upon Process Goals

Age	Current Proficiency	Process Goals												Practice		Tournaments, Leagues and Programs
		Having fun	Making friends	Learning life skills	Physical exercise	Skill development	Developing endurance	Regional competitive experience	National competitive experience	Skill improvement	Mental toughness	Travel opportunity	Skill mastery	Weeks per year	Hours per week	
11 to 12	Beginner	X	X	X	X									6	2	USA Team Tennis (Youth) – Red Stars
	Intermediate	X	X	X	X	X								12	2	USA Team Tennis (Youth) – White Stars / White Stripes
		X	X	X	X	X	X	X						44	2	SCTA – Satellite / Open
	Advanced	X	X	X	X		X	X		X				44	2	SCTA – Open
		X	X	X	X		X	X		X	X	X		44	4	SCTA – Open / Designated
		X	X	X	X		X	X	X	X	X	X		44	8	SCTA – Open / Designated USTA – Levels 3 to 1

Table 5.3 *(continued from previous page)*

Choice Table – Part 2 of 2
Sample Format to Pick the Right Tournament Based Upon Process Goals

Age	Current Proficiency	Tournaments, Leagues and Programs	Near-term Desirable Outcomes															
			Recreation	Social benefits	Fitness	Understand match rules	Earning a sectional rank	Top 10 sectional ranking	Earning a national rank	Sectional endorsement	Top 10 national ranking	Earning a sponsorship	Making the high school team	Earning a college scholarship	Making the national team	Earning travel grant	Making the college team	Turning professional
11 to 12	Beginner	USA Team Tennis (Youth) – Red Stars	X	X	X													
	Intermediate	USA Team Tennis (Youth) – White Stars / White Stripes	X	X	X	X												
		SCTA – Satellite / Open	X	X	X	X	X											
	Advanced	SCTA – Open	X	X	X		X		X	X								
		SCTA – Open / Designated	X	X	X			X	X	X								
		SCTA – Open / Designated USTA – Levels 3 to 1	X	X	X						X	X						

Periodization

Sports scientists use the fancy term "Periodization" to tell you to your face that your 14-year-old is not going to be able to play her best in each of the ten or so tournaments in which she is registered to play this year. Attempting to train the hardest and play the best every day of the year will only lead to injury or burnout, or both.

That's not to say every now and then, the player should have a cavalier attitude toward training or take matches lightly. Periodization is about finding an appropriate balance between physical training, drills, match play, and rest so the player reaches a peak level of performance at a calculated time.

Experts recommend picking one or two important tournaments from a player's yearly schedule and planning a 12- week periodization training around the competition, weeks 9 and 10 being the tournament weeks.

Say the player wants to devote 10 hours to training in a week, a typical periodization schedule would be as shown in Table 5.4.

Table 5.4

Hours	**Week 1-to-5**	**Week 6-to-8**	**Week 9-to-10**	**Week 11-to-12**
Physical Training	3	1.5	1	3
Drills	3	2.5	1	2
Match Play	3	5	7	2
Active Rest	1	1	1	3

The weeks after the tournament are called a period of active-rest. The player should rest for a few days immediately following the tournament. Later, the player can engage in light training in order to keep in shape, including playing other sports in addition to tennis.

At first glance, this schedule may appear impractical. Come on, what kid would want to drill and train the week following the Super Nationals? However, the junior should be encouraged to stick to this schedule as much as possible. She will thank you for it when she decides to join the professional tour, where mental and physical demands are much greater.

Tournament Travel

Teenage players love competitive tennis because it gives them a chance to travel independently. At the higher echelons of junior competition – intersectional, national, and the international circuit – a portion of the travel tab may even be picked up by the USTA.

Itinerary

There are hundreds of junior tournaments so it shouldn't be difficult to find nearby tournaments for a beginner or intermediate level junior player. As a junior advances in the rankings race, tournament travel is inevitable.

Crisscrossing the country, traveling overseas, meeting new people, and learning about other cultures is both fun and educational. But a junior has to be prepared to live out of a suitcase for periods of time because the schedule can get hectic.

Housing

If a parent chooses to accompany the child, they might stay with friends or in a hotel. Even if the tournament is within a three to four hour drive from home, it may be advantageous to arrange an overnight stay so the player is better prepared for her match. Tournaments sometimes offer recommendations and discount deals at hotels near the tournament site.

Tournaments may also offer private housing and transportation, including airport transfers for all players who live more than 50 or 60 miles from the tournament. Players can stay at the homes of other players or with members of the host club. In this case, the host family assumes responsibility for providing meals, local transportation, and general supervision. Often, tournaments may pitch in by providing lunch and transportation to and from the tournament site.

Most tournaments carefully screen host families, but it is a good idea to verify this with the tournament director. A player who stays with a host family should be instructed to behave appropriately so the visit is a pleasant experience for both the host family and the player.

Doubles Partner

Choosing the right doubles partner is in some ways like picking a business partner. Good chemistry, integrity, and skills that complement are important factors.

Besides playing with her partner, your junior will be spending time before and after the match with that partner, traveling to tournaments, and maybe even lodging together. Obviously, having a partner that she can get along with easily is nice in general, but can also help junior stay relaxed before matches.

Kids sometimes go overboard trying to win a game. Making bad line calls on purpose is one example. If a partner develops notoriety for bad on-court behavior, it reflects poorly on the team. It may call for intervention from friends and parents and, in extreme cases, may even require a change of partners.

Next, look for a player with a complementary game – in strokes and strategies. A player with a strong backhand and so-so forehand may want a partner with a powerful forehand. A player whose style is to try many winners should partner with a consistent player so the ball is kept in play until a winning chance becomes available. A professional coach could judge these qualities and suggest some potential partners.

After all these qualities have been met, select the highest-ranked doubles player one can find. Junior is more than half way to winning her next doubles match.

Tournament directors will sometimes help players find a doubles partner if the player is unable to find one, especially in a new town. Getting to know the new partner off-court will help the doubles game and this initial personal interaction might just blossom into a lasting friendship.

Advice for the Tennis Traveler

Dear Miss Marta:

Our family recently vacationed at a posh golf and tennis resort. When checking out, the front-desk attendant inquired, "Did you enjoy your golf, Sir?" I appreciated the courtesy but was irked that she assumed I had been golfing when, in fact, my wife and I had enjoyed a week of great tennis on the courts of this beautiful resort. I disguised my annoyance and politely replied that we did a lot of tennis and enjoyed it very much, thank you. I think it is discourteous to assume only golf is played at a golf *and* tennis resort. What do you say?
– Irked in Scottsdale

Miss Marta says: Where do resorts find such addle-brained dollies? Blow off some steam. Write a letter to management but spare the front-desk person. It could be the training – or lack thereof. Now, go hit some balls.

♣♣♣♣

Dear Miss Marta:

I would like to know how your readers feel about an online trend I find disturbing. I surfed into a resort reservation web site in hopes of planning my tennis vacation. Under the activities menu, the web site listed golf, scuba diving, skiing, fishing, and so on. Tennis was nowhere to be found! I think tennis is as much an "activity" as golf and scuba are. Tell me you agree.
– Peeved SurferGirl

Miss Marta says: The online company got what it deserves. No business from you. Zilch. Nada. You go girl!

6

Match Time

"To know how to do something well is to enjoy it."
PEARL BUCK, writer.

Little things can add up when it comes to making those long hours of practice payoff on match day. For instance, knowing the tournament rules and code of conduct is a good idea. Checking equipment the previous evening and getting a good night's rest can make a difference on the big day. Arrive at the tournament site early and well fueled and always complete a proper warm-up routine.

Translating Practice to Match Play

When top juniors turn professional they discover in a hurry that even an early round match is played at a level many notches above anything they have ever faced. Juniors who practiced at a level beyond those needed to win the next junior tournament – over-practice – are usually the ones who can make a smooth transition from junior competition to the professional level.

From the 12s to the professional levels, periodically, it's important to raise match play practice up a few notches. Arrange practice with a partner who's at a higher level and encourage the junior to give it everything he's got. Every now and then the junior should play a long practice match and play as if life depended on it.

Practice to win against a player whose big weapon, say a kick-serve, is every junior's nemesis. Develop a signature stroke and over-practice it – a killer volley for doubles, or forehand groundstroke for singles. It's good to have a shot to depend on when stakes are high. Practice playing safely in the heat, serve with the sun in your eyes, and attempt a win in windy conditions.

Match day can present many new factors to worry about – a new town, an unknown opponent, or a school assignment that has to be turned in the next day. Over-practicing on a periodic basis can help junior relegate basic strokes, techniques, and conditions to the subconscious. Being more "in-the-zone" allows a player to maintain his natural level of play, in spite of normal distractions and nervousness.

For key tournaments like the season-ending Sectional Championships, break away from the normal practice routine. Instead, develop a specific practice plan leading up to the championships. A coach may suggest a daily routine alternating between grooving a specific shot in one session, practicing winning a serious match the next, followed by a conditioning session, always with adequate rest periods in between.

Preparing for the Match

You won't find professional players who party all night long and head straight into a match early the next morning. If they do, it's guaranteed they won't be on the professional circuit for long. There are pre-match rituals most players follow so they can do their best.

At the same time, match preparation does not have to be a regimented boot camp. Rather, it is a set of simple, easy-to-follow routines, like getting a good night's sleep the night before match day. When parents encourage the child to follow a pre-match ritual it becomes a habit. Soon the child will start to prepare for the match without bring prodded.

24 Hours Before Match Day

Most tournaments inform players of their match times by email, posting on the tournament website, postal mail, or even by phone. It's a good idea to reconfirm the start time with the tournament desk a day before the match. Tournaments have mandatory time penalties: being five minutes late costs the player one game; ten minutes late costs two games and fifteen minutes late costs three games. Show up more than fifteen minutes late and it will cost the player his match.

Maintain a high-carb diet, especially when facing a long, grueling match: whole-grain breads, cereals, and pasta, plus plenty of fruits and vegetables. Avoid fat and spiced foods. In the same way you encourage your kids to put homework and stuff in their school backpack before going to bed, help them prepare their match bag with rackets, spare shirt, and so on the day before a match. And don't forget the MP3 player with all his favorites.

Get as much sleep as possible the night before a match. Sometimes this is a challenge because of travel or the proverbial butterflies in the belly the night before an important match. Children need to know that it's okay to lose sleep once in a while. More important is that they not psyche themselves out before a match because of lost sleep.

Fueling for the Match

Go bananas, go nuts; salad with chicken; peanut butter crackers; non-sugar cereal; potatoes and pasta – yummy. All easy-to-prepare or out-of-the-box foods that a busy parent can offer to ensure the kid is well fueled on match day. The high-carbohydrate plan helps store glycogen in the muscles and liver as fuel for activity. Once again, avoid high-fat and spicy foods.

Eat three to four hours before reporting time so food is completely absorbed from the stomach. At the tournament site a light snack of portable foods ought to keep junior happy. Fun and healthy snack ideas include trail mix, happy face rice cakes, ants-on-a-log celery sticks, fruit juice popsicles, mini-bagels, and fruit yogurt.

Kids don't sweat as much as adults do and are less able to cool off. They also absorb heat more easily. These factors increase the risk of dehydration in kids. Give children a squeeze bottle of water or sports drink and remind them to take gulps before, during, and after the match. A sports drink is tasty, will supply energy, and turns on thirst, encouraging kids to gulp frequently.

Match Day

For afternoon matches, taking a cat nap, playing board games with friends and family, or getting a massage from the on-site masseuse are all great ways to achieve some calm before the storm. If little junior has an early morning match, parents ought to help him wake up at least a few hours before the competition. You don't want a groggy junior sleep-walking to the court.

Get to the tournament site 30 to 40 minutes before reporting time and check in at the tournament desk. In the early rounds, the tournament desk can provide only an approximate start time for matches. A new site and the hustle and bustle of parents, players, coaches, and officials can be intimidating for a young child. Fill up waiting time by getting to know other parents and players. Many lasting friendships have blossomed at tournament sites.

If the coach is available, an older kid may like to discuss the game plan, or perhaps set up a short 15 to 30 minute hitting session on a practice court to loosen up the muscles and groove in a specific shot.

Before the Match

Quiet time. Famous basketball coach Phil Jackson had his players take a ball into a locker room corner and visualize the game plan. Don't expect your little bundle of energy to do that just yet, but make room in the schedule for some quiet time so you establish a good pre-match ritual for later years. The MP3 player or a handheld game may do the trick.

About 15 minutes before match time head to the tournament desk for the court assignment. Get to the court for warm-up. A few minutes of thorough stretching will loosen up the muscles for the match and go a long way in preventing long-term injuries.

It's a good idea to get the heart rate going by running around the court and doing some sideways sprints. Hit some warm-up shots with the other player. Professionals recommend starting with the best stroke, but don't forget to hit all the other shots, too, in order to get in the groove. At match time, prepare to win.

As a junior develops, competition days will increase. There will be travel to tournament sites in different cities and countries. Travel is an exciting perk for a tennis kid, but acclimating to a new city and culture takes some getting used to. Following a standard set of pre-match rituals will reassure the junior that every match is, in fact, like any other, allowing relaxed and focused play.

Etiquette

Good etiquette is not snobbish behavior. It's simply a way to allow everyone involved in a social gathering to have a good time without hindrance. Translated to a tennis tournament setting, good etiquette means players, spectators, parents, and coaches accept certain behavioral norms so that everyone, including you, can derive maximum enjoyment from the match.

Parent Etiquette

- Until a kid can pack her bags and fly to a tournament all by herself, the parent has to help junior prepare the match bag the previous night. On match day, get her to the tournament site in plenty of time so she doesn't feel rushed and is ready for her match.
- Resist the temptation to sit in the most visible seat, hemming and hawing and tearing your hair at every point your kid loses. Officially called "one-of-those," parents who do this are an annoyance to other spectators and to players as well.

- Try and cheer good points made by both players. Cheering a little louder for your little angel is perfectly acceptable!
- Don't hesitate to have your child removed if she is misbehaving on the court. No match is more important than teaching a child life lessons.
- No matter the outcome, hug your child as she comes off the court.
- Should you bump into the parent of the other player offer to buy the family a soft drink and get to know them. If the two families live in different cities, the kids may choose to stay in each other's homes during tournaments, and it's always beneficial to develop an acquaintance. Michael Chang's family hosted Pete Sampras and Andre Agassi during their junior years, beginning a lasting friendship.

Coach Etiquette

Adhering to social graces guarantees an all-round enjoyable match, whether one is a certified coach or a parent who proxies for the coach.

- In most tournaments coaching during a match is banned, so don't. Some team competitions permit coaching under very specific rules.
- Record observations, but do it unobtrusively, without distracting the players.
- Hug your junior after the match, regardless of the outcome.
- Put off talk about the match until later, much later, perhaps even the next morning, to give the kid a chance to cool off emotionally. With very young kids, instead of talking to them about mistakes and improvements, simply make mental notes and incorporate appropriate changes into their lesson plans.

Spectator Etiquette

- Switch the *@#*@# mobile phone to silent mode. Step outside the spectator zone if you must make a call and do it during changeovers.
- Don't yell or call the ball while the ball is in play.
- Wait for a changeover to get in or out of the bleachers.
- Go nuts when your favorite player wins!

Player Etiquette

The USTA publishes a book called Friend at Court (More info: usta.com). It is perhaps the best reference there is to acquaint a tennis family with regulations and the code of conduct for players.

The book covers, in excruciating detail, the many aspects of player etiquette, for example, when to call the score; what to do when you doubt a call; how to handle disagreements, and so on. It's worth every word, because court behavior is an important building block in a junior's character.

Here's the rest of the story on player behavior:

- On court, wear that beautiful smile as often as possible, but avoid the antics professionals put on for television.
- Caution the other player when you're about to return balls to her for serving. This is not the way to take out your opponent.
- Acknowledge an opponent's good shot with a tap of the racket or nod of the head.
- If you couldn't see a call, ask your opponent if she saw the ball. If so, allow her to make the call. If she didn't see it either, make the call in favor of the opponent.
- Do jump up and down crazily after a victory, but always remember to congratulate your opponent on a wonderful game and thank the officials. Pick up balls after the match.

During the Match

While junior dukes it out on court, there is a lot a coach and parent can observe. A professional coach will go about his business, making notes on technical stuff like serve percentages, points won on first and second serve in, aces, return errors, winners, and points won at net.

There are many handy tools available to a coach who wants to do more than make mental notes. Tennis workbooks, handheld personal digital assistants, electronic tennis data recorders worn like a wristwatch, and the good old scratch pad are all worthy aids to record observations.

Instead of getting all wound-up worrying about match results a parent can observe two factors over which he has the maximum impact – on-court behavior and mental toughness. Is junior displaying good player etiquette? Are there aspects of junior's behavior that need to be discussed with her the next day?

When looking for mental toughness observe whether junior is incorporating habits that sports psychologists recommend:

- Focal point: Concentrate on the ball when it's in play. Between points focus on a specific object – the racket strings, the ball. One of the first coaching tips Nick Bollettieri gave Anna Kournikova was to ask her to avoid looking up at her mom after every point.
- Service ritual: Develop a ritual before any point – sweeping hair back, bouncing the ball before serving. Follow the ritual regardless of the match situation.
- Breathing: Learn to exhale on contact, which can establish a breathing pattern for emotional control.
- Loosen-up: Enhance relaxation by loosening the hand and thigh muscles, carrying the racket in the non-dominant hand, and stretching.
- Posture: Even if a player is behind on the scoreboard she needs to communicate resiliency through body language – shoulders pulled back, head high, and striding with a purpose.
- Self-talk: Avoid negative self-talk and berating after a mistake.

There are a variety of established drills that work on mental toughness. Discuss observations with the coach and determine whether appropriate mental drills can be incorporated into lesson plans. If you suspect family or school issues may be affecting the ability to concentrate, try and get to the bottom of the problem as soon as possible.

After the Match

Following the match, junior should thank the other players and officials. If there is another match to be played, get a schedule from the tournament desk. It's important to refuel immediately. Research suggests that consuming carbohydrates within 30 minutes of exercising helps reload muscles within 12 to 16 hours.

Once again, win or lose, remember to hug your child. It's natural for parents and coaches to want to talk about everything they observed during the match. Allow an older child a few hours, or even overnight, before talking about the match. You will find a better listener when you do analyze the match. Focus on the process, not the result. For instance, instead of discussing a low first-serve percentage, talk about whether the serve-toss was off.

For a young child it's best to simply appreciate his effort and plan other post-match activities away from tennis. Visit a health juice bar, for example. Discuss observations directly with the coach and have them incorporated into lesson plans.

Learning from a Match

Tennis players are on their own in a match, usually without the help of coaches or teammates. Two factors are extremely important to keep them playing and improving. The first is self-motivation achieved by entering tournaments that give the player a chance to maintain a win-loss ratio of at least 2 or 3 to 1. The second factor is self-learning. Winning is important, but win or lose, a player has to come away from a match with a "Eureka!" feeling of having learned something significant.

Self-learning in tennis is an acquired skill. This means a coach or parent has to teach a junior how and what to learn from a match. Lynn Miller, Varsity Tennis Coach at Wheaton College, has developed a simple and practical tool to help high school and college players learn by evaluating their match play.

The Match Profile Data Form (Table 6.1) is designed to capture self-rated scores in five areas – wins, fitness, mental toughness, life skills, and a new area added in the form here, enjoyment. Scores are based on criteria suggested in the form and are on a scale of 1 to 10, with 10 as the best.

All areas except wins are based on subjective guidelines. For example, if a player is in mediocre shape he would rate his fitness 5 or 6; mentally tough, although not perfect, give yourself 8 or 9; displaying outstanding sportsmanship, give yourself 10 for life skills.

The Match Evaluation Form (Table 6.2) asks players to think about their match with respect to strategy and tactics. Lynn Miller suggests players talk to the coach before filling out this form. Question #7 is of the utmost importance because it takes the player past understanding of what happened to the action phase.

Be wary – no one enjoys filling in forms, especially kids. Play becomes "work." Perhaps limiting the paperwork to certain practice matches and tournaments may be one way to make use of this system go down a little easier. Rewards for turning in the forms can help. Stir up your creative juices and judge when and how to get your junior involved in this process.

Table 6.1

Match Profile Data Form Maximum score for each category is 10. A total of 45 or above is commendable. Discuss the completed form with your coach.					
Wins	Fitness	Mental Toughness	Life Skills	Enjoyment	Total
Wins: Games won divided by games played. Example: If the score is 6-0, 6-2, then 12/14 multiplied by 10 = 8.75. Rounding off gives a wins score of 9.					
Fitness: Did you feel "strong" on the court, were your feet constantly moving? Were you repositioning after each shot? Were you reaching short balls on balance and recovering quickly for overheads? Were you able to stay in long points physically and recover well for proceeding points? Did you have enough energy to breathe out audibly on most shots? Did your diet impact the match? Did you train appropriately with adequate intensity/rest ratio?					
Mental Toughness: Ability to recover from adversity. Ability to demonstrate strong body language and use of positive imagery. Exhibiting a "never give in" attitude with maximum effort. Demonstrating a love of the challenge and the game. Being able to keep track of the score. Playing the "big points" with strategically sound judgment.					
Life Skills: Treating all opponents with respect. Standing up for what you believe to be true when challenged. Learning steps for conflict resolution. Not taking your opponent's personal problems as directed at you. Keeping your actions in perspective. Setting an example for others to follow. Your ability to generate support for your teammates.					
Enjoyment: How memorable was the match for you? How strongly do you desire to repeat your match performance? How relaxed were you?					

Table 6.2

Match Performance Evaluation Form		
MATCH #:	YOUR NAME:	DATE:
COMPETITOR'S NAME:		
1. RIGHTY OR LEFTY:		
2. STRENGTH:		
3. WEAKNESS/VULNERABILITY:		
4. HOW YOU PLAYED THEM:		
5. YOUR MOST MEMORABLE MOMENT:		
6. WOULD YOU DO ANYTHING DIFFERENT NEXT TIME?		
7. ON-COURT DRILLS YOU'D LIKE TO PRACTICE BEFORE PLAYING THIS PERSON NEXT TIME:		

The Match Profile Data Form, used along with the Match Performance Evaluation Form, shows high school and college players how to reflect on their matches in a constructive manner and helps them decide what steps they need to take to progress to the next level.

7

Camps and Resorts

"Just play. Have fun. Enjoy the game."
MICHAEL JORDAN, professional basketball player.

Kids Camps may bring back fond memories for grown-ups, but probe kids today and you'll be surprised. They either love 'em or hate 'em; there is no in between. If parent and child do their homework before selecting a camp, there's a much better chance the child will want to go back the next year.

Benefits of a Tennis Camp

Tennis-wise perhaps the most important benefit of a week of workouts for a young kid is the discovery of what it takes physically to compete in a tournament, playing matches round after round. Kids also get plenty of practice partners with different abilities – some superior, others equal, and still others who are relative rookies.

An advanced player can focus on executing a particular strategy, improving a specific stroke, or correcting an error. It's not uncommon for a tournament player to pick up a new doubles partner from among his new friends at camp. Learning from a different coach, even for a week, may open up new perspectives on the game. Often, a kid used to playing recreational tennis returns from a week of fun with friends at camp eager to take up competitive tennis.

Some camps include talks by experts on topics like mental toughness, physical conditioning, nutrition, strategy, and tournament play. And don't forget the evening activities – trips to the beach, barbecues, camp dances, and more.

Choosing a Camp

With over 200 tennis camps conducting nearly 800 weeklong sessions each year for kids, making a short-list is the first step in choosing a camp. Start with online directories (More info: shawguides.com; juniortennis.com; and tennisresortsonline.com) and books: "Tennis Camps, Clinics and Resorts" by Joanie and Bill Brown and "The World's Best Tennis Vacations" by Roger Cox.

The online directories are generally more up-to-date and easier to search and shortlist. However, keep in mind they are simply listings and are neither authenticated nor accredited.

The American Camping Association (ACA. More info: acacamps.org), founded in 1910, is an association of camping professionals that works to create a model and standardizing influence in organized camping for the young. The ACA has currently accredited over 2,400 camps.

The ACA accredits camps based on an educational process, providing training and publications for camp directors and staff. At least once every three years, an outside team of trained camp professionals observes the camp in session to verify compliance with over 300 health, safety and program standards.

As application for ACA accreditation is voluntary, unfortunately, you won't find many tennis camps, even the high-quality ones. Hopefully, with more awareness about the ACA's role, this should change.

Meanwhile, the best way to decipher a camp's character is with an in-depth conversation with its director. Try to determine whether the character and program emphasis are a good fit with your child's personality. A reserved child might do better at a camp that emphasizes instruction over competition, while a star player would probably prefer a camp that offers plenty of competition.

Happy Campers

The number of returning campers is the best measure of camp quality. There is currently no way to determine return rate statistics for the tennis camp industry. But don't be shy about asking the director of a camp you're interested in what the return rate is. Quality camps will proudly share these statistics. Avoid camps that waffle over sharing this kind of information.

Instructors

Forget the camp director. Find out who is actually going to instruct the kids. Are the instructors certified professionals or college tennis players? If they're college players, make sure the director will closely monitor progress and the quality of instruction.

It's beneficial when the schedule includes rotation of instructors for different drills. The students can pick up a variety of tips. As in most tennis clinics, the ideal student-to-instructor ratio is four to six students for each instructor. Too low a ratio can tire or bore the students, while too many can result in a free-for-all.

Tournament Tough

Kids preparing for intersectional and national tournaments may want to pick camps with court surfaces that are different from the ones on which they usually practice. Many camps offer a variety of surfaces. The Westside Tennis Club in Houston, for example, features all four Grand Slam court surfaces.

Getting used to wind and weather is a big part of becoming tournament tough. Advanced players from New England may want to practice playing in a Florida camp, where it will often be sunny, hot, and humid.

Evening Activities

Many kids will want to return to the camp the following season because of the evening activities and camaraderie. Campers enjoy first-run movies, skits, dances, and a trip to the town or beach. If your child is shy, find out if the camp has specific getting-to-know-each-other activities.

Accommodations

Dorm is the norm as many camps are held on college campuses. The glitzy ones go for the cottage theme. Either way, a great roomie and a decent sack are all kids really care about until the early morning rise-and-shine knock on the door.

More Money

A one-week resident camp can run you from $500 to $1,000 plus. Day camp is a little more than half as much. The resident camp price includes lodging, meals, instruction, use of facilities, and evening activities. Don't assume a bigger sticker price means better instruction. Generally, the higher price buys better accommodations, easier access, cutting edge facilities, or simply a popular brand.

Despite all the detective work, you may discover the camp you chose isn't a good fit, after all. A camp is more than the tennis it offers. The social atmosphere is also important and that can be hard to figure out beforehand. It might take more than one try to find the best match for your child.

Brand Name Camps

The choice is easier when we limit the shortlist to famous brand names. The professional brands, such as Bollettieri, Van der Meer, Vic Braden, and the corporate brands like Nike all evoke perceptions of what to expect at those particular camps.

For instance, the Bollettieri camps are known for the get-tough bootcamp style, while Van der Meer's students swear by the effectiveness of his "standardized" method of teaching. An efficient stroke based upon scientific research is the Vic Braden way.

Expecting a celebrity coach to greet you at the camp entrance is about as likely as expecting Sam Walton to wave customers in at the nearby Wal-Mart. Occasionally, celebrity coaches do bop in on sessions. But mostly they impart their experience and techniques through a camp system of trained teachers, methods, and teaching philosophy that mirrors the master's way. So even though you may never meet Vic Braden at a Vic Braden camp, rest assured you will benefit from the master's signature, writ large in all aspects of the camp.

Kids' tennis camps bearing the names of well-known professionals and corporations include:

- Bollettieri Tennis Academy (More info: imgacademies.com).
- Van der Meer Tennis (More info: vandermeertennis.com).
- Vic Braden Tennis (More info: vicbraden.com).
- John Newcombe Tennis Ranch (More info: newktennis.com).
- Hopman Tennis School (More info: saddlebrooksports.com).
- Evert Tennis Academy (More info: everttennisacademy.com).
- Nike Sports Camps (More info: ussportscamps.com).

Unlike the professional brand name camps, each of which practices a uniform method of instruction at every location, corporate camps bear the local director's personal stamp.

Making Camp Count

Most camps accept children as young as age 6 or 7. You can gauge a kid's camp readiness by how well they handle sleep-overs with friends. Young children will be less homesick at camp once they have gotten used to sleep-overs.

Camp sessions can run four to five hours of on-court time. A kid practicing tennis year-round may be physically conditioned for such an intensive schedule. Otherwise, players ought to get acclimated through a conditioning routine that begins two to three weeks prior to the start of camp. That way your kid stays healthy and injury-free during camp.

Nike camps encourage campers to write down short- and long-term goals and to decide how they will go about reaching the short-term goals while at camp. Experts recommend making self-evaluation notes at the end of each day. Campers can rate themselves on their level of effort, attitude, responsibility, willingness to take risks during games, focus, improvement, and of course, on how much fun they had that day.

It's also a good idea to encourage kids to make notes about camp memories – their accomplishments, tips they learned, and contact info for all their new friends. Finally, kids should go home and practice what they learned at camp.

Tennis Resorts

A week's vacation at a nice tennis resort can help a player get away from it all, yet keep the bearings greased for the upcoming season. Food, scenic location, cost .... blah, blah, blah and blah. But just as important are the tennis benefits the resort has to offer your tennis kid.

A one-on-one session with a resort pro might just be the best way to introduce tennis to a young child, but only if it's lots of fun. The child will then associate tennis with all the other fun activities that were part of the vacation. It can't be said enough that "fun" is the best magnet to keep her enthused to learn the sport.

And speaking of fun, the PBI Tennis Show held at some tennis resorts is an extraordinary event for both the young and the young-at-heart. Developed by Peter Burwash, the show is a sophisticated production serving up an eclectic mix of music, humor, slick racket and ball control skills, and educational tips on the game. The PBI Tennis Show has been called "The Harlem Globetrotters of Tennis".

Peter Burwash also places trained coaches at tennis resorts all over the world. A resort with a PBI professional assures a well-defined tennis program for guests of all ages and levels of proficiency (More info: pbitennis.com).

The fun activities offered by resorts, combined with regular hitting sessions in a relaxed setting, can reinvigorate a competitive kid. Working with the resort Pro, even for just a few sessions, will often yield a fresh evaluation of a kid's game. Some resorts, like the Marriott Desert Springs in Palm Desert, offer all three surfaces – hard,

Time Out

David could not wait to spill the beans. His company had named him "Salesperson of the year" and awarded a two-week, all-expenses-paid vacation for him and his family at a nice tennis resort. He was sure his 10-year-old tennis kid, Alex, would jump with joy. The kid loved the game and had been attending regular tennis lessons for nearly a year.

So David was perplexed when, after making the big announcement at the dinner table, Alex paused for a moment and asked with apparent concern, "Do I have to attend tennis clinics?" It suddenly dawned on David that although Alex enjoyed tennis, the resort was simply more of the same for him. A vacation should offer a break from the routine.

David assured Alex that the resort had plenty of other programs and amenities for kids, like waterslides and a Kids Club. When they got to the resort David and his wife signed up for the tennis clinics, while Alex pursued other activities.

The clinics, under the tutelage of the resort's excellent Pro, proved to be a lot of fun. On the fourth day of the family's vacation, Alex asked if he could come along to watch his parent's clinic. At the courts, Alex made friends with the Pro and everyone at the Pro shop. By the end of the clinic, Alex was asking, "Dad, can I play, too?"

David broke into a smile and with mock firmness replied, "Son, I can hit a few balls with you now. Maybe we ought to reserve a court for ourselves tomorrow." With that, David let Alex bump the balls for a few minutes before they both headed for the pool.

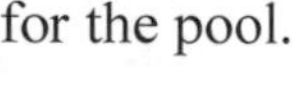

clay, and grass.

There are a plethora of options available when choosing the right tennis resort. Consider whether the resort offers the following:

- A trained and certified Pro.
- Well-attended clinics for all age groups.
- A variety of court surfaces.
- Player matching service. Parents who play tennis will find the service that matches up players for friendly hitting sessions a welcome feature.
- Professional and amateur tournaments. Resorts often host tennis tournaments. A week of watching a WTA challenger event, combined with daily clinics, is a great idea.
- Fun activities like the PBI Tennis Show and the Club Med Circus.
- Cost-saving tennis packages. These packages offer room rates that include daily tennis clinics in the morning and ball machine practice in the afternoon.

In addition to using the resources of your travel agent and the many online travel sites, you can also find books specializing in tennis vacations: “Tennis Camps, Clinics and Resorts” by Joanie and Bill Brown, and “The World’s Best Tennis Vacations” by Roger Cox are two great sources of information. You can also search the online resort guides (More info: tennisresortsonline.com and pbitennis.com).

Just about every good hotel in the world located in a “sunbelt” has tennis courts, and every tennis-loving family can find places to play tennis on vacation. However, resorts specializing in tennis serve up a unique experience somewhere between the “total immersion” of a camp and the do-nothing solitude of a beach pad.

8

Gearing Up

"I'll let the racket do the talking."
JOHN McENROE, professional tennis player and television analyst.

A minimalist can perhaps enjoy tennis for a lifetime with just a racket and balls. But show me a kid who's a minimalist and I'll sell you the Brooklyn Bridge for zilch. Make stuff interesting, they'll enjoy playing a whole lot more.

Rackets come in all sorts of appealing designs. You can buy a racket unstrung and have it strung with different colored strings and paint a personalized logo. Balls come in combinations of bright colors. Tennis apparel for tots can be no less snazzy. The clothing featuring wisecrack phrases always seems to bring a smile to onlookers. A braided headband can be an inexpensive touch to make your tennis gal look and feel special.

Virtues of Value

Your little princess has just got to have that tennis diva's trinket she saw on television. Well, if you can get hold of an affordable kid version, why not? After all, looking the part adds to the allure.

Rackets, however, are different. Younger kids outgrow rackets in about a year so value shopping makes sense. Get an idea of the price range by browsing online stores. Follow your mom's smart shopper advice. Stay away from the highest priced rackets for beginner play – you usually pay for the brand name anyway. Eliminate the cheap ones, too. A racket that looses stiffness quickly or with improper balance can lead to injury. Go for middle-of-the-road priced rackets.

You get what you pay for in ball-machines, though. The pricey models provide a whole range of bells and whistles, features you will use at one stage or the other of your kid's tennis development. Repairs can be expensive, so think seriously about adding the extended warranty if one is available.

Your kids will undoubtedly want the really cool shoes and statement clothes. So why not establish a way for your junior to earn them? For starters, those tried and true chores like mowing the lawn or babysitting will do the trick. Tennis outcome-related rewards for young kids are a definite no-no. “Johnny, you can have those cool shoes if you beat Brandon in the finals today.” This is a sure recipe for disaster.

Instead, reward your 8-year-old for getting to practice on time. For a 10-year old, how about avoiding junk food for a week? As your junior develops and becomes a competitive player, offer to buy those cool shoes when he completes an endurance drill or achieves a 60 percent rate of first serve.

Rackets

The racket is a junior’s most important piece of gear. A correctly fitting racket helps junior learn the right techniques and minimizes the risk of injuries of the wrist, elbow, and shoulder. So don’t skimp on taking time to pick the right one.

Here’s the Number One Tip for buying a junior racket: have your kid shop with you. You’ll want to know three of his measurements:

- Height (H)
- Arm length, armpit to fingertips (A)
- Tip of ring finger (i.e., fourth from thumb) to the first long crease on the palm (T)

At the pro shop, while your kid wanders the aisles wide-eyed in the company of Agassi, Capriati, and Mickey Mouse, make your move. This is your chance to make the most important choice of gear for the junior.

Use Table 8.1 to gauge racket length, the longest end-to-end measurement. Select the measurement that gives you a longer racket.

Table 8.1

Height (H) feet-inches	**Arm Length (A) inches**	**Racket Length* inches**
3-10 or less	21 or less	21
3-11 to 4-5	23	23
4-6 to 4-11	25	25
5 or more	27 or more	27 or longer

* Source: Tennis magazine

If your kid is five feet or taller, he's an adult as far as rackets are concerned. Celebrate! While length and weight determine swinging comfort, a racket has to be comfortable to grip, too. Use measurement T to gauge the best grip circumference. Junior grips start at three inches. Four inches and above are considered adult-sized grips. If the length is right but the grip size is less, ask if an overgrip can be taped on to make the hold more comfortable.

Whew. That's enough math for the moment. Now that you've short-listed a few of rackets with the correct length and grip, in your price range, bring on the champ. Let the kid pick from your short-list. Chances are, it will be a cool-colored racket or one emblazoned with Mickey Mouse, Scooby Doo, or Andre Agassi. Go ahead and make his day.

Remember, kids tend to outgrow rackets very quickly. Plan to buy a new one every year, or even a little more often. Relax, medium-priced rackets range between $20 and $50. As a junior moves to adult-sized rackets and competitive play, you will probably buy fewer rackets, but you may need to buy more than one at a time. Two rackets is the absolute minimum for a competitive player. It's not uncommon to break a racket during play, and even more common to break strings during a match.

When your junior is able to rally and serve consistently, you can consider other factors when buying rackets, such as head size, frame stiffness, and string elasticity. A tête-à-tête with your junior's coach is invaluable because many of these factors depend upon style of play. For example, midplus heads (90 – 105 sq. in.) are preferred for serve and volley type games. Oversized heads (110 – 135 sq. in) are best suited for baseline and doubles players because the extra area helps to add spin and provide more area to hit the ball.

Racket Care

When you learn that there exists a select group of people called Master Racquet Technicians (MRTs) dedicated to the maintenance of rackets, you realize that caring for rackets is not for the faint of heart. The good news is that up until middle school, junior will probably be outgrowing rackets every year.

The only way a new racket can be ruined is by leaving it exposed in a car. A comfortable temperature for your racket is 60 to 80 degrees Fahrenheit. The temperature inside a car parked in the sun can easily rise to 140 degrees, warping the frame and depleting the strings.

A thermally insulated racket storage bag is a worthwhile investment indeed.

It's easy to understand why good strings are essential for peak performance. Jump on a concrete slab. Now jump on a trampoline. Which do you suppose will take you higher? The wear and tear of play causes strings to lose their elasticity and develop notches over time.

When the junior begins to use her racket over longer periods, have an MRT restring it with a good replacement string. This returns power and control to her game and extends racket life. Replacement strings are available for under $10 and a string job can be had for $30.

The MRTs at the United States Racquet Stringers Association (USRSA. More info: racquettech.com) recommend that a player have rackets restrung the same number of times per year as they play per week. That means a player who plays three times a week should restring three times per year.

Check the grip condition when restringing. If the grip is worn, there is greater chance of racket twisting, which can cause arm problems. Replacement grips are inexpensive. They come with perforations to channel sweat away and gel strips to absorb shock.

Putting on a replacement grip is a simple do-it-yourself job. Start by wrapping the tapered end around the butt (bottom of handle), then work your way up the handle. Don't overlap or leave gaps as you go. Right-handed players wrap clockwise; lefties, counterclockwise.

Foot Care

Lleyton Hewitt, at 5 feet 11 inches, is diminutive compared to the average pro. He has no single stroke weapon. Yet he can dominate his opponent simply because he gets to the ball quicker than anyone on the court. Footwork is so crucial in tennis.

Shoes

Do we need fancy footwear? The start and stop motions, as well as the quick direction changes involved in tennis require special features in footwear. A well-designed tennis shoe is durable enough to protect against overuse injury and light enough that it doesn't interfere with agility and performance.

Running and cross-training shoes don't provide the lateral support so essential for tennis. They put feet high off the ground increasing the chance of ankle rollover. Brand name tennis shoes may be expensive, but they're a safe bet against tennis injuries. Look for shoes with flat bottoms for balance on court.

Many players drag their toes, especially when serving. A toecap on the shoe enhances durability. Herring bone-style tread wears slower and offers more traction than the raised checkerboard styling of multi-purpose shoes. Grass court shoes have different treads than those used on hard courts.

Experts recommend replacing shoes every six months or so, even if the tread doesn't look worn out. The mid-sole that provides cushioning can become soft or spongy.

Socks

There are more sweat glands on the feet than anywhere else on the body. A drenched sock can cause chafing and blistering. Athletic socks wick away moisture keeping feet dry. Socks should also provide cushioning at the toe and heel. Pick low-cut socks when your little girl wants to make a fashion statement.

Insoles

Pete Sampras suffered from shin splints some years ago, caused by the foot rolling inward and straining the lower body. This can also lead to Achilles tendonitis. Sport insoles and inserts can cradle and support the foot, preventing inward rollover.

Apparel

Regular school sportswear is fine during the early years, until your junior decides she wants to pursue tennis as one of her primary sports. Then it's time to give in to your little angel's pleas for the Maria Sharapova look, right down to the trinkets on her wrists and ear lobes.

You can find tennis apparel in junior sizes 4 through 16, mainly at your local pro shop and online stores. The variety is mind boggling for girls. Tops can be cotton-based polos, tees, and tanks with micro-fiber skirts and unisex shorts. Dresses work well, too. Many designs come with attached spandex shorts underneath, with a pocket to tuck a ball for second serve. The shorts and dresses are also available separately. Boys will have their tees and polos with daring logos. Check for pockets in boy's shorts.

Head to Toe: Accessories

Accessorizing is fun. Some, like the tiara for girls, are just for fun; many are useful and quite a few are indispensable. Remember when Serena Williams dropped her shining tiara on court? That was a code violation. So if your little girl wants to show who's the princess on court, be sure to lodge the tiara firmly.

Hats and Visors

A regular baseball hat works fine to keep out the glare and protect skin from the sun. How about a visor to give both protection and show-off highlighted blonde locks?

Sunblock

Slather it on 20 minutes before play. Check out the sweat proof varieties, like Coppertone Sport SPF 30 sunblock, designed especially for athletes. Remember mom's advice on sun protection: "*Slip* on loose clothing. *Slap* on a wide brimmed hat. *Slop* on sunscreen."

Bands

Boys, they got bandanas to make a fashion statement. Headbands help keep sweat and wet hair out of players' eyes. How about braided ones for girls? Wristbands prevent sweat from running into the racket handle. Use wristbands for wiping a wet forehead. Look for bands with a mixture of cotton and lycra spandex.

Vibration Dampeners

This is a small shock absorber inserted between the strings near the throat of a racket. A vibration dampener may limit the repetitive stress that causes tennis elbow. Besides, they look cool on a racket. Who knows, a neon green worm-shaped dampener or the "red eye," a red ball-bearing floating in a viscous liquid, may well be the talk of the locker room.

Racket bags

Organize all that tennis gear with a racket bag. These bags come in two, three, and even six racket sizes. Besides making your junior look like a serious tennis player, they're invaluable for protecting rackets from the heat. Manufacturers offer a variety of bells and whistles on these babies: zippered pockets to tuck away membership cards, keys, overgrips, and other valuables; compartments for wet shoes and clothes; and pockets for a mobile phone and water bottle.

If you're lucky enough to have bike access to practice courts, how about a racket backpack? The pouch is designed so the racket stays angled away from the back of the head. Besides space for shoes, jacket, and water bottle, you may want one with an internal Walkman holder and headphone pass-through. Neat-o!

For juniors on tour, consider a rolling racket bag on wheels with telescoping handle, toiletry compartment, and garment bag hook.

Balls

Manufacturers use ball sales to gauge the growth of tennis throughout the country. With the HEAD/Penn Company making over a quarter of a million balls every day, tennis must be darned popular. Of course, the short lifespan of a tennis ball might have something to do with it.

A typical pressurized ball lasts no more than three to six sets of play, or three hours of practice. Once the ball can is opened, a stored ball looses bounce and plays dead within three to five weeks. A dead ball ruins learning and can cause tennis elbow problems. How do we determine when the ball is dead? Drop the ball from 100 inches onto a hard court. The regulation bounce back is 53–58 inches. If the bounce is substantially lower, trash the ball.

Balls may well be the big-ticket item on your tennis list, as they have to be constantly replaced. Fortunately, the permanent-pressure or pressure-less practice ball is an option. These last from one to two years when used in ball machines and teaching carts and can be bought by the bucket for substantial savings. Be sure to revert to pressurized balls in the weeks leading up to a competition, as these are the only ones official tournaments use.

Practice balls are also available in bright two-tone colors, in addition to regulation yellow or white. A yellow-blue ball may be perfect for teaching spin. The colors help your junior see the rotation on the ball.

Court Equipment

There are various kinds of equipment that can make practice sessions more fruitful. If your junior plays on public courts, the parks and recreation department may be willing to provide a metal shipping container you can use to stow equipment overnight.

Ball Hopper

Inexpensive wire-frame bins are great for storing up to 100 balls and can also be used for carrying, picking up, and feeding balls during practice. The wires at the bottom load the balls into the hopper for convenient pick up. The handles can be flipped down to become legs, morphing the ball hopper into a feeding cart.

Roller ball hoppers are equipped with a wire drum instead of a bin. Pick up is easy compared to the wire-frame relative, as the hopper picks up balls by rolling the drum. They can carry over 150 balls.

Ball Tube

Tennis players hate picking up balls. All that changes when you hand out a bright orange ball tube to a 6-year-old. Kids can't wait to tear away from the drill and scurry around tubing the balls without having to bend down to pick them up. Plastic ball tubes hold 20 balls.

Mini-nets

Introduce tennis to your peewee with a portable mini-net. These are 10 to 17 feet long, cost less than $100 and can be set up on your lawn in seconds, without tools.

Round out your equipment inventory with a sweep roller that dries the court after an overnight shower.

Training Aids

Can't find a practice partner for your junior? How about buying him one? Actually, how about buying two? A ball machine and a rebound net will do the trick. Most training aids are available directly from the manufacturer and from tennis catalogs or online tennis stores.

Ball Machine

The ball machine can blast balls every five seconds, up to 95 mph with varying spins and trajectories. Hitting with a ball machine is a great way to achieve focus, stroke consistency, and endurance. Most prices range from $500 to $3,000.

The new generation of programmable machines have taken capability to a new level. These machines can be programmed to toss a sequence of strokes of any type, in any order – flat, lob, topspin, and slice. These models can also place each ball in a variety of specified locations on the court.

Of course, bells and whistles come at a price. High-end machines are priced for clubs and run about $6,000-plus. So if you belong to a club, you might be able to nudge the club into buying or upgrading to one of these new-generation ball machines.

When Andre Agassi was still a teenager his dad set up a few ball machines on their backyard court. Look where it took Andre. Be forewarned, though, if you have courts in your own backyard and decide to emulate this tactic. Some machines use air pressure to fire balls and can be quite noisy. You do want to be a good neighbor, don't you?

If you're using public courts, you can find many portable models that run on batteries, weigh less than 50 pounds, and fit inside the trunk of a car.

Rebound Net

When your junior wants to practice on the driveway, buy him a portable rebound net and save your walls. The net offers a 7-foot diameter target area and a lively spandex-generated rebound. Setup is easy and requires no tools.

Air Target

Create a 3-foot by 3-foot air target with this lightweight PVC frame. Place the target along the singles sideline to practice down-the-line passing shots, or move the frame to the middle and work on crosscourt shots. Since the trainer is three feet above the net, hit over it for depth.

Ground Target

These come in lots of shapes, sizes and colors – rubber cones, donuts, spots, arrows, and ropes in bright yellow, orange, or green. Mix and match the targets and colors and your junior is guaranteed to have loads of fun training with ground targets.

8 Board®

This is a poly-carbonate board in the shape of a figure eight, about the length of a stride, that is adjustable, with swiveling circular footrests at its ends. The inventor of this product, Jack Broudy, who is a certified tennis professional, says the board develops correct fluidity of body movement that results in strokes with more power and control.

Match Play Bag

So your 11-year old is rearing to graduate from clinics and beat the stuffing out of his competitors on the junior tournament circuit. Before you let your little bull loose in the china shop, teach him how to prepare his bag for match play.

A carefully stocked bag will help your kid perform his best. Here are the top essentials:

1. Two rackets.
2. A can of balls.
3. Water: Athletes can sweat half a gallon each hour. Don't just sip water, drink it.
4. Fuel: Energy bars, a bagel, and a banana can bring back the zip, especially when playing two matches.
5. Towel.
6. Bands, sweatband and headband.
7. Hat or visor.
8. Sunscreen.
9. First aid: Chemical ice for cramps and band-aids to deal with blisters.
10. A spare shirt: A shirt change can help a player look and feel comfortable again.
11. Extra socks.
12. Post-match change of clothes.
13. Money.
14. Mobile phone.
15. Paperwork: Membership card, tournament information, USTA's Official Rules of Tennis and Code of Conduct booklets.
16. Leisure stuff: Walkman, Gameboy, or a novel for rain delays.

Brad Gilbert of "Winning Ugly" fame carried Jolly Rancher candies. Mark Philippousis stuffs airline tickets in his match bag. See if your kid can add to the list with an item uniquely his.

Fun Stuff

A 9-year-old from Tacoma, Washington wrote the pastor of the church: *"Dear Pastor, I think more people would come to your church if you moved it to Disneyland."*

While kids love to hit balls, getting kids interested in physical conditioning is a challenge. Luckily, quite a few companies are introducing fun products with just this goal in mind.

Z-Ball

These rubber balls have knobs on them that create unpredictable bounces. They're great for building dexterity and hand-eye coordination.

Aeroprops

Get them by the dozen to increase tracking and catching skills and for just plain fun. Aeroprops are little plastic wings that soar as high as 50 feet and are easy and safe to use, even for the very young.

Finger Yo-Yos

Put on a Finger Yo-Yo the size of a tennis ball. Bounce and retrieve to develop rhythm or practice serve tosses.

Jump Rope

This is one piece of equipment your kid is guaranteed to have fun with through adulthood. Look for adjustable ropes in durable plastic, with cushioned handles. Jumping rope improves agility, balance, and strength.

Frisbee

You can mimic Lleyton Hewitt's conditioning routine to develop explosive strength by running short sprints on the beach, or you can throw and chase a frisbee.

Power Ladder

This is a 30-foot ladder you lay on the ground. Drills such as hopping in and out of each rung improve foot speed, quickness, balance, and coordination.

Best Buy

Imagine this. For a game that can be enjoyed with a racket and a couple of balls on a parking lot, a la Andre Agassi in a World Team Tennis promotion, tennis stores are lined with literally thousands of specialty items. Finding the best racket or shoe for your kid may not be easy, especially for parents new to tennis. Getting advice from a coach who works with kids can save you time and money.

Sporting goods chain stores rarely carry the range of items you need to explore. A specialized tennis store or a local pro-shop may be your best bet, more so for first-time buyers. You can find pro shops in tennis clubs and resorts, staffed by knowledgeable folks. Many also have stringing machines, nice to know when you need that racket restrung.

Online stores can be great for research, repeat purchases such as replacement shoes, balls, and the latest-and-greatest accessories. Many tennis-only mail order catalogs have been in business for decades and are run by dedicated tennis enthusiasts. They supply all the usual tennis stuff, as well as innovative training aids.

Tips from the Pros

Besides picking up on Maria Sharapova's trinkets, juniors can learn from what the top pros wear and wield on court. Check out your favorite player's racket and attire. Granted, what players use and wear are influenced by endorsement deals and there's no guarantee that junior versions of these brands will yield equivalent performance. But it is certainly safe to assume that professional players would not risk playing with an inferior racket simply because it meant a better endorsement deal. All the same, it's interesting to keep tabs on who's wearing and wielding what.

Future Gear

Mike Agassi, Andre's dad, says that a big challenge for parents and coaches raising tennis kids is trying to predict the state of the game 10 to 15 years from now and attempting to tune training to what comes next. A big part of predicting the game's evolution is to analyze where the racket will be, technologically, years from now.

While manufacturers attempt to enhance stroke power with racket technology, the smart folks at the ITF and USTA, folks responsible for equipment standards in the United States, are determined to uphold the human element.

In the future, according to Tennis magazine, rackets will have sensors that will keep a tally of your stroke statistics, accessed on a tiny LCD screen during changeovers, like on-court coaches. Technologists at Wilson predict the synthetic strings amateurs use will increasingly perform like gut, which top pros use today. Strings will be lodged in replaceable cartridges and when a string breaks, instead of grabbing another racket, the player would simply snap in a new cartridge.

Shoes? Well, they'll be at least 40 percent lighter than they are now, with soles that re-channel impact energy back to you for a bounce effect.

Who knows what the future holds? Though one thing is certain about the future of tennis gear. Rackets won't ever hit the shot for you, not in tennis.

A Letter to Santa

Dear Santa:

Merry Christmas. My name is Tyler. I am 7 years old. How are you feeling today? My favorite thing to do is video games. My favorite color is blue. My favorite thing to play is tennis.

Last week I played tennis for the first time. Tennis is fun. Yesterday my dad and I went to a bookstore to buy some books on tennis. We asked the nice person at the desk for help finding tennis books. He led us to a back corner of the store and pointed to a single shelf at the bottom.

How I wish they could carry more tennis books, and put them in a better place so they're easier to find. My dad and I bought a few great books on tennis. Dad talked to the store manager about how hard it was to find the tennis books in his store and told him there weren't very many of them either. The store manager thanked my dad for talking to him. He is a nice man. He gave me a lollipop.

Santa, I have tried to be good this year. I am giving two of the tennis books we bought to my friend Joe because his family doesn't have the money to buy gifts this Christmas. I know there are lots of kids in the world who don't have the money to buy such wonderful books. Could you please give tennis books to a poor child for me?

Thank you,

Tyler

9

Physical Conditioning

"You can never do too many sit-ups."
MATT RANKIN, swim coach.

Playing tennis regularly is a great way to keep fit for life. However, participating in other physical activities is also important. Pediatricians say that from middle childhood to early adolescence is the time to acquire and develop sport-specific skills.

Participation in a variety of sports and developing an exercise routine outside of tennis will help strengthen different muscle groups. Risk of overuse injuries is reduced and, in many cases, all-around conditioning improves tennis performance.

Scientific studies have validated, again and again, what the Greeks taught us about the mind-body connection. Physical fitness has a beneficial effect on academic performance.

Academic Achievement

Wanna become a better reader? Try doing some push-ups. A statewide study conducted by the California Department of Education (CDE) matched the reading and math scores with the physical fitness scores of nearly a million students in grades five, seven, and nine.

Announcing the results, the CDE's Delaine Eastin said, "This statewide study provides compelling evidence that the physical well-being of students has a direct impact on their ability to achieve academically." Students with high scores in fitness also scored high in reading and math. Furthermore, students who met minimum fitness levels in three or more of the six physical fitness areas showed the greatest gains in academic achievement at all three grade levels.

Reading and math levels were assessed using the Stanford Achievement Test (SAT-9), given as part of California's Standardized Testing and Reporting Program. The study used a physical fitness test known as Fitnessgram (More info: cooperinst.org) to assess health in six areas – cardiovascular endurance, percentage of body fat, abdominal strength and endurance, trunk strength and flexibility, upper body strength and endurance, and overall flexibility. A score of 6 indicates that a student is in the healthy fitness zone in all six performance-areas, and meets standards to be considered physically fit.

Tennis Performance

As Alex Corretja and Carlos Moya battled on court, a battery of networked computers were quietly tracking the players' every move on court in the finals of the ATP Tennis World Championships in Germany a few years ago.

The visual processing system called LucentVision concluded that each player had traveled six miles at speeds reaching up to 18 mph during the five-set match. Considering that world-class athletes sprint at 22 to 23 mph, incredibly, for Corretja and Moya, the match was like sprinting six miles.

Being in good physical condition not only helps a player last the match, in many cases a fit player will be able to get to the ball quicker, hit with more power, and recover faster, making him a better competitor. Good conditioning also ensures one can enjoy the game for a lifetime by reducing the risk of overuse injuries.

Sports scientists from the USTA and University of Connecticut tested over 80 ranked 8 to 12-year-old boys with a suite of physical performance tests (More info: Select References 3). The purpose – examine the contribution of physical abilities to tennis performance, specifically to the rankings. The investigation found that agility – the ability to change direction quickly – was the first physical characteristic to influence competitive ability in this age group.

The study further hypothesized that other physical factors like endurance, strength, and speed will also begin to influence tennis performance as kids attain physical maturation, usually after 12 years for boys and 10 years for girls.

Participation in Other Sports

Perhaps the easiest way to ensure all-around conditioning is to encourage little Jill to play other sports. This is especially true for the under 14s, who may more willingly commit to participation in other sports as opposed to working out at the gym.

Adding variety is a fun way to achieve total body conditioning and avoid the burnout caused by tennis-all-the-time syndrome. Certain sports can even help improve tennis performance. Swimming and cross-country skiing are perhaps the best sports to achieve total body conditioning. Inline skating and dancing also offer conditioning benefits.

Hockey, both ice and field forms, are great for coordination and provide vigorous workouts. The volleyball serve is similar to the tennis spin serve. Boris Becker developed his explosive footwork playing soccer until the age of 12. During his professional days, Becker often invited his coach, Nick Bollettieri, to join him in a vigorous basketball session. Basketball offers benefits in the areas of conditioning, footwork, and coordination.

Think you should start yoga only after hitting 40? Think again. Encourage your pre-teen to hit the mat and she'll continue to thank you well beyond her 40th birthday. Yoga reduces the risk of long-term injuries by increasing flexibility and strength of the joints. It can also help sharpen focus during a match. And speaking of focus, how about Bruce Lee-style martial arts for concentration and a healthy dose of assertiveness training, so necessary to win matches.

Not all sports complement tennis, though, and some sports can actually hurt tennis development. Playing baseball may develop a higher backswing and upward tilt to the tennis racket. As a result, groundstrokes will often end up outside the court. Golf can also cause a high backswing. Racquetball is too wristy compared to tennis.

How about chess to improve on-court tennis strategy? Dubious choice, eh?

Making Exercise Fun

Kids get bored when they're told to exercise as a means to an end, in this case better tennis performance. Instead, consider exercise an end in itself – make it a fun activity the child looks forward to for its own sake. Double the fun by joining in.

Shoot hoops on the driveway one day, play frisbee after a day or so, and bike the next. Twirl around with a hula ring. Looking for a fun activity that will more directly impact conditioning for tennis? Skip rope. Boxers have the fastest feet in the world and skipping is a major component of their training. It's also an unbelievable workout that demands control, endurance, speed, coordination, and strength.

Add variety by choosing a new activity for each season. Try sledding, skiing, or snowboarding in the winter, swimming or in-line skating during the summer, hiking and biking in the spring and fall.

Take a routine task and make it a fun activity for parent and child. Walking Fido, for instance. Develop a routine of walking the dog together. It's simple, but it works.

Measuring Fitness

Using masking tape, mark on the court a hexagon with two-foot sides. The athlete stands in the middle of the hexagon facing out. Upon the command "Ready-Go," start the stopwatch; the athlete jumps forward over the tape with both feet and back to the middle, again with both feet. Continuing to face forward, the athlete jumps over the next side and back again. Stop after three full revolutions of the hexagon and record the time.

The Hexagon test (More info: Select References 4) is designed to rate the athlete's agility – the ability to change direction quickly, a critical skill for tennis. Developed by USTA Player Development, the Hexagon is one of a battery of tests designed to identify the junior's baseline fitness.

The tests cover flexibility, strength and power, body composition, speed and agility, and aerobic capacity. Obtaining a current fitness profile every three months or so helps the player train more efficiently and design a custom fitness program that not only improves tennis performance, but can also reduce the risk of injuries.

The USTA has produced a video entitled Fitness Testing for Tennis (More info: usta.com) that shows tennis instructors and coaches how to administer the fitness testing protocol. The video narration by Dr. Jack Groppel begins with a cardiovascular test and warm-up routine. Next, viewers learn step-by-step how to perform each of the tests. The video also lists all of the equipment needed for each test and shows how to properly record the test results.

Another more generalized fitness assessment protocol called Fitnessgram, which we briefly discussed earlier in this chapter, has become the choice of thousands of schools for the annual physical performance testing of their pupils. Developed by the Cooper Institute (More info: cooperinst.org), the primary goal of the Fitnessgram test is to help students make physical activity a part of their daily lives.

Flexibility Training

Flexibility refers to the range of motion in a joint and its related muscle groups. Flexibility training increases the length and elasticity of muscles, reducing the risk of tearing a muscle when chasing down balls.

Though most kids are naturally flexible, a regimen of stretching for five or ten minutes before and after tennis goes a long way in preventing injuries. More importantly, forming a habit of stretching will pay dividends as they grow older and their bodies become less flexible.

It's not uncommon for eager kids to rush into tennis drills as soon as they're dropped off for practice. If the coach is not including a warm-up routine at the start of every practice, it is the parent's responsibility to arrive five or ten minutes early and go through a warm-up routine with the child. A cool-down stretch after class is important, too.

Use "funny talk" to get kids motivated. For instance, stretching the quadriceps muscles in the front of the thigh is a core component of any warm-up program. This involves raising one foot behind you and bringing your heel to your butt. Naming this routine "The Stork" is a fun way to help kids remember it.

Depending upon your child's situation, it may be wise to enroll in a flexibility training class such as yoga or Pilates. Flexibility aside, these programs improve agility, increase strength without bulking up, and work on the mind-body connection. There are lots of great videos and books on stretching, yoga, and Pilates produced by specialists. Educate yourself and be sure to consult with your child's pediatrician before starting any physical training program.

Building Strength and Power

Young children don't have to take a class in strength training. Simply encourage them to play outdoors. Soon they'll be climbing trees or enjoying a swim in the backyard pool – activities that make the muscles work against resistance; they'll also be building muscle and increasing bone density.

Body-weight Exercises

Bones continue to harden during the growing years. Up until adolescence the area at the ends of long bones consists of soft cartilage known as growth plates. Near the end of the adolescent period the growth plate is replaced by bone.

Experts say strength training exercises that involve light weights can be introduced around adolescence. Body-weight exercises – squats, lunges, push-ups, pull-ups, crunches, resistance-band exercises, rope-climbing, and light weights with lots of repetitions are safe.

Manual resistance exercises use a partner to develop strength. These exercises add variety to a workout and significantly increase the number of exercises available to the young athlete.

Interval Training

It may surprise you to know that a long-distance runner who can endure a marathon won't last through a vigorous tennis match. Unlike slow distance workouts, tennis requires repetitive bursts of intense energy alternated with longer durations of normal activity.

During short bursts of activity, the body uses energy stored in the muscles – glycogen and ATP. The by-product is lactic acid, which is responsible for the burning sensation we feel in our muscles during strenuous workouts. During periods of normal activity, the heart and lungs work together to break down any lactic acid build up. In this phase, oxygen is used to convert stored carbohydrates into energy.

Training for this form of repetitive activity, called interval training, leads to the adaptation response. Muscles develop a higher tolerance to the build-up of lactate. The body begins to build new capillaries and is better able to take in and deliver oxygen to the working muscles, thus strenghtening the heart muscle. These changes result in improved performance.

After a gradual warm up, start running, moving at about 70 percent of your maximum speed. Hold this pace for about a minute. Then slow down to your normal tempo for two minutes. Increase your speed again to 70 percent for another leg-exploding, lung-expanding minute. Cool down to a relaxed pace for another five.

Playing frisbee in the park is as good as any interval training involving running sprints. Use intervals for walking, running, cycling, or in-line skating. If you don't relish watching the clock, simply speed up between streetlights.

Plyometrics

"Plyometrics are exercises that enable a muscle to reach maximum strength within a short time," says Dr. Donald Chu, a leading authority on power training and author of more than half a dozen books on Plyometrics, including "Plyo Play for Kids."

Plyometrics training enhances a kid's ability to increase speed of movement and improve power production. The exercises start with a rapid stretch of a muscle followed by a rapid shortening of the same muscle. There are many injury-proof Plyometrics drills designed for kids using soft cones, medicine balls, and other accessories. Common games that kids play such as skipping, hopscotch, and leapfrog; jumping jacks, bunny hops, and certain moves in aerobic dance are all forms of Plyometrics.

Light Weights

Bulking up like a weightlifter is not helpful for tennis, but adding a few pounds of muscle can greatly enhance one's ability to handle pace and hit more powerful shots. The goal is to increase muscular and bone strength while retaining flexibility and movement.

Use light dumbbells, resistance bands, and other free weights with lots of repetitions. In consultation with a fitness trainer or coach, design a variety of strength training routines including wrist curls and sawing. The general recommendation is to introduce weight training after adolescence.

Good Eats and Body Composition

You are not only what you eat, but also how much you eat. Most parents and coaches have become very aware of the importance of a well-balanced diet with healthful portions of proteins, fats, and carbohydrates.

Competition demands even more attention to good nutrition. Eating right the night before a match and three to four hours before reporting time will keep the player's energy high on the court. Energy foods rich in carbohydrates are solid fuels – lots of brown bread, potatoes and pasta, pancakes, bagels, raisins, and bananas. Refuel with similar high-carb foods one to two hours after the match. Never forget the importance of regular hydration. Choose sports beverages or plain old water.

Supplements

The scientific community has finally proved the efficacy of vitamin supplements. A multivitamin, antioxidant, and mineral complex are now an athlete's essentials.

Teenagers develop special nutrient needs as they experience tremendous growth spurts and hormonal changes. Individual likes and dislikes, as well as peer pressure can contribute to poor diets. Because of their eating habits and special nutrient needs certain food supplements may be useful.

Avoid supplements formulated to optimize hormone levels including testosterone and growth hormones because they may interfere with natural growth patterns. Meal replacement shakes and powders may sometimes be the only hope for a rushed teenager, but limit their use and seek medical advice before using these products.

Body Composition Tests

To be sure all that healthy eating is paying off, two simple tests are available to determine body composition – Skinfold and Body-Mass Index. A parent or fitness trainer can perform these tests. The results provide an estimate of a child's percentage of body fat when compared to body mass composed of muscles, bones, and organs.

- Skinfold Test: Using a basic device called a skinfold caliper, measure the thickness of the skinfold on the back of the upper arm. Use this measurement with the Skinfold chart to obtain body fat percentage (More info: cooperinst.org).
- Body-Mass Index: Based on height and weight measurements, a BMI table will provide an index number. The index will tell you if the child's weight can be considered healthy, overweight, or obese (More info: cooperinst.org).

Speed, Agility, and Quickness

Speed is how fast a player covers ground; agility is the efficiency in changing direction; and quickness is the ability to get off the mark. Watch Lleyton Hewitt in action and you soon realize that these three qualities are his greatest assets. A player good in all three departments – speed, agility, and quickness (SAQ) - will be able to reach even the most well-placed shots.

A tennis player runs an average of 9 feet per shot and a total of 24 to 36 feet in the pursuit of a single point. Breaking down tennis movements – forward movement occurs 47 percent of the time; sideways movement occurs 48 percent of the time; and backwards occurs 5 percent of the time (More info: Select References 5). SAQ training for tennis players should be performed over short distances and focus on the development of both lateral and linear movements.

Basketball and ice hockey most closely approximate tennis movements. A season enjoying either sport is a natural way to improve SAQ ability. Interval training and Plyometrics exercises that involve sideways and forward-backward movements are also good for SAQ improvement.

Many tennis coaches incorporate SAQ training in warm-up routines. Happy feet, crossovers, ladder drills, pattern runs with cones, and line drills will all have your kid chasing down balls like never before.

Try this basic SAQ drill for fun. The parent or coach stands about two yards away with a tennis ball in his hand, held at head height. He drops the ball to the ground. The child's goal is to react as soon as the ball leaves the hand and catch the ball before it bounces a second time. Increase the distance and you'll increase the challenge.

Aerobic Capacity

Performing a physical activity for a long time without getting breathless requires good aerobic capacity. Keep in mind that the teen years are the most important time to develop aerobic capacity.

Although over 70 percent of a tennis match consists of short bursts of intense activity, aerobic capacity is still important for tennis players. Short bursts of intense activity produce lactic acid that is associated with premature fatigue. During long and hard rallies lactate levels can double. In these situations, experts suggest, sufficient aerobic capacity is needed to remove the lactate build up, thereby increasing endurance.

Swimming laps, doing step aerobics, and jogging are all activities that will improve aerobic capacity. For tennis-specific training, instead of long runs, focus on interval training. Alternate between reaching maximum speed and reverting to a normal pace.

Injuries

No pain, no gain. A little discomfort is part of any sports and fitness routine. For a muscle to become stronger it must experience a higher than normal load. This slight overload is perceived as "the burn" and is the "good pain" necessary for improved performance. Onset of fatigue is another sign that activity is pushing the limits.

Good Pain, Bad Pain

The discomfort associated with "good pain" is short-lived; it should not persist for hours or days. With rest, the slight fatigue should also go away.

Certain pain, though, lasts long after exercise. It affects sports performance, functions outside of sports like walking, sleeping, shaking hands or getting dressed, and does not go away after rest. These are examples of the "bad pain" one should always be concerned about. Discourage your child from playing through pain. Seek medical evaluation right away if pain persists.

Sometimes kids are less than honest about disclosing the real nature of their pain, either because they want to compete in an important tournament, attain a certain ranking, or make the team. The best antidote for this behavior is talking to the child about pain and injuries before they occur. Explain how to distinguish good pain from bad pain. Tell them why they need to be honest with you and with themselves about the "bad pain." Make them understand how timely care of pain and injuries will enable them to enjoy the sport for a lifetime.

Common Pains

Pains associated with shoulders, elbows, and knees are common to tennis. The parent, coach, and player should all keep an eye out for this kind of "bad pain." At the first sign seek medical advice.

Tennis elbow is an injury associated with pain on the outer side of the elbow. Any combination of repetitive rotation of the wrist while using force can cause tennis elbow. The most common causes are:

- A one-handed backhand stroke where the elbow leads the racket head until just before impact, causing use of forearm snap at the last minute.
- Improper grip size.
- Vibrations from a tightly strung racket.

Making simple adjustments can help to avoid tennis elbow. Keep the racket head ahead of the elbow during backhands. Turn sideways and step into the ball with the front foot. These adjustments will reduce the stress on your forearms. Proper grip size, string tension, strength training for wrists and forearms – all these are factors that reduce the risk of tennis elbow.

Court coverage and changing direction on hard courts can cause problems in knee joints. Charging the net, lunging to return a serve, and chasing down a drop shot require strong legs. Exercising legs with squats, lunges, and stair-climbing will go a long way in strengthening them.

A vicious kick serve can earn a quick point, but repetitive use of such serves and overhead shots without appropriate conditioning can tear the tendons that connect the shoulder and arm. Shoulder pains can be avoided by adequate warm-up of the shoulder area prior to playing tennis and strength training that concentrates on the shoulders.

Healthful Habits

The problem with most sports injuries is that you won't know you have them until joints become tender and you start to feel pain. Rehabilitation usually requires extensive treatment and rest. Once again, it is important to educate your child on good pain versus bad pain. Help him understand the importance of practicing good habits that will help prevent injuries that can appear, without notice, years later. Here are some healthful tips:

✓ Overall fitness is the best way to avoid injuries. Pay special attention to the demands of tennis and those parts of the anatomy that are not worked as much by tennis alone – strengthening the legs, forearms, shoulders, and stomach.

✓ A cardio routine, followed by stretches before any workout and another few minutes of cool-down stretches afterward, is essential.

✓ Always wear proper tennis shoes. Cross-trainers and running shoes are big no-nos for tennis.

✓ Use uniformly good balls. Mixing good balls with bad ones will throw off a player's timing and strain the elbow and knees.

✓ Have racket grip size and string tension checked by a racket technician on a regular basis.

✓ Never play through pain. Seek medical attention right away and rest as many weeks or months as the doctor advises.

✓ Drink plenty of water during workouts.

✓ Have an extensive physical examination by a doctor every six months or so. This is invaluable for competitive players.

✓ Play with proper strokes – early preparation, racket back, holding the elbow close to the body; hip rotation, and weight transfer through the ball; contacting in front and keeping the racket head above the wrist at contact.

✓ Rest. Take frequent time-outs from vigorous physical activity of any kind.

The National Youth Sports Safety Foundation (NYSSF. More info: nyssf.org) and the Sports Medicine section of the National Federation of State High School Associations (NFHS. More info: nfhs.org) are two sources of current information regarding safety issues in sports.

Conditioning Roadmap

You can find loads of scientific research, books, videos, and television programs that discuss the nuts-and-bolts of physical conditioning. It's easy to get carried away. Educate yourself and keep current but remember to avoid too much structure at a young age. Keep conditioning simple and balanced. Above all, make physical conditioning enjoyable for its own sake. Jogging along a beautiful trail beats the treadmill hands down.

A balanced conditioning program will include training for flexibility, strength, power, speed, agility, quickness, and cardio. Incorporating all these elements in routines appropriate for your tennis kid can be challenging. Table 9.1 provides a general roadmap that can help. Personalize the roadmap depending upon your child's physical growth and level of tennis intensity.

Consult your child's doctor and a certified trainer before starting any physical training regimen. Complete physical examinations, by a doctor, once or twice a year are a must.

Table 9.1

Age	Physical Conditioning Program
Under 13	Make a habit of doing warm-ups before tennis. Start with cardio and follow up with stretches. After tennis, perform a cool-down routine.
	Incorporate age-appropriate conditioning drills during tennis lessons. Drills that focus on speed, agility, and quickness are best.
	Participate in a variety of sports in addition to tennis. Achieve beginner-level proficiency in at least one sport in each group: • Swimming, skiing, snowboarding, dancing for all-around conditioning • Ice hockey, field hockey, basketball, soccer
	Allow time for unstructured outdoor activities.

Table 9.1 *(continued from previous page)*

Age	**Physical Conditioning Program**
14-15	Add light structured training, selecting at least one from each group: • Yoga, martial arts, and other flexibility and mind-body workouts. • Body-weight exercises, Plyometrics, interval training, light weights, and resistance bands are good for strength and power.
16 plus	Hire a fitness expert and develop an individualized conditioning program.

Most schools have physical education classes. In California, students in grades 7 through 12 participate in more than three hours of physical exercise each week. Factor in such hours of exercise when designing a program for your child. You can find after-school sports and fitness classes at health clubs, YMCAs, junior camps, and community centers.

Happy moving!

A Letter to Santa

Dear Santa:

Hello, my name is Dina. I am 6 years old. I have a big brother named Jamie and a dog named Buddy. I want to know some things about you. Do you have children? Are your reindeer ready for Christmas Eve?

Yesterday I went to an exciting tennis tournament with my family. My big brother was playing in the tournament. We had a lot of fun, but now I am sad. You want to know why?

A whole bunch of kids played in the tournament. By the end of the day, all but one of them were "losers" because there was only one winner. My brother played his best but lost in the third round, so calling him a "loser" makes me sad. I wish, he could be called a "second-round winner" by the people in charge.

Wouldn't it be nice if we could say there was a "first-round winner" rather than a "second round loser"? Maybe new kids who lose in the first round can be called "competitors." That's a big word I learned from my brother. I also heard that some tournaments have something called "lucky losers." I don't think that sounds very good either.

My mom explained to me that in soccer, the people in charge changed the words "sudden death" to something that makes you feel better – "golden goal." Tennis tournaments are so much fun. I wish we could also have them celebrate every player's hard work. We should get rid of the term "loser" and take it out of the rulebook, too, don't you think? Santa, could you bring me a Cinderella toy, and for my brother a new tennis dictionary?

Lots of love,

Dina

10

Mind Games

"Tennis is 90 -percent mental, the other half is physical."
Adapted from YOGI BERRA.

Mental conditioning can be an emotional boot camp, but it doesn't have to be. When incorporated into routines like tennis practice at an early age and fostered gently, mental conditioning can become a tool not only to develop a better tennis player but also a better person.

Mental fitness includes three key components: mental attitude, emotional toughness, and mind-body coordination. Mental attitude can be nurtured on court by the coach and off court by the parent. Emotional toughness and mind-body coordination develop naturally with tennis training, but if you want to up the ante, consider training in martial arts or yoga.

Parent as Mental Coach

A parent can make perhaps the most important contributions to a child's tennis development in three ways – by acting as a mental coach; by actively encouraging off-court physical conditioning; and by playing regularly with the child.

Mental coaching does not have to be complicated or time consuming. A simple insistence that the child smile and shake hands after a tennis match sends a number of positive attitudinal messages. This behavior helps the child learn relaxed play and to de-emphasize wins and losses, a critical component of the development phase.

The handshake also means the player is thanking the competitor for allowing him to give his best effort. The focus of competition is shifted away from beating the other player to challenging the child's own potential and reinforces the desire for continued improvement.

Choosing an appropriate time to coach your kid on the mental aspects of the game is important. You want to make sure he's an effective listener. If his mind is pre-occupied, you'll get an impatient nod or an "I know, I know." Talk to him during non-tennis activities. A good time might be during exercise or while walking the dog.

Reinforce those discussions with gentle reminders as you drive your kid to class. "Johnny, remember the other day we talked about how to stay focused on the point? Try to keep your eyes on the logo of the ball throughout a point." Ideas stay fresh in his mind and the kid can implement them and see how they work for him.

Here are a few questions to stimulate a lively discussion with your child. Just laying it out there will often work wonders with mental attitude and preparation. Put on your psychologist's cap and become a mental coach:

- What is the true nature of competition? Is competition a threat or a challenge? Can competition help improve your game? How can competition help you become a better person? How is amateur competition different from professional competition?
- Little Johnny has won the championship two years in a row, why is he still afraid of competition? Could it be because expectations are too high? What should Johnny do to stay relaxed and enjoy the challenge?
- Jill is facing off against her best friend, Ashley, in the next match. Jill plays better than Ashley and wants to win. Yet she doesn't want to hurt her friend's feelings. Can Jill reconcile this dichotomy and approach the match prepared to win?
- The Jill and Ashley match result reads 6-3, 6-4. The pair's previous match was 6-1, 6-0. Can Ashley find redeemable qualities in her performance and truly feel she's a winner at different levels?
- At what stage of tennis development are skill development and effort more important than the result of the match?
- Do you compete to please yourself, your parents and coach, or both? Why is playing for your own enjoyment important?

On-court Mental Conditioning

At one time or another, most players have been victims of nervousness, choking, and even tanking during a match. These difficulties are all symptomatic of other, underlying causes. For example, nervousness and choking may be the result of worrying too much about the end result of the match.

"The greatest players I have seen in my decades of teaching are those who forget the past and don't think about the future," says legendary teacher Vic Braden. "Their only concern is the shot currently being hit." Learning to focus on each point and being in the "here and now" is a big part of on-court mental training. What about the time between points? The mind has to be trained to utilize this free time positively.

Awareness

Forget the previous stroke. There's probably a lot happening right now that demands the player's attention – the sun, wind, spin of the ball, trajectory, feel of the racket, movement and positioning of the body, breathing, and the target area. "Awareness is everything," says Phil Jackson, professional basketball coach. Learning, playing, and enjoyment all greatly improve when we teach the mind to stay interested in the here-and-now.

The challenge for a coach is how to teach kids to be more aware. Mental fitness skills are not easily imparted by just talking to kids. Merely lecturing them to stay focused and aware will not work. The skills must be woven into drills and activities.

Perhaps the best way to habituate kids is via Timothy Gallwey's awareness drills. First presented in his seminal Inner Game classic, the drills and modern-day variations have become part of the standard repertoire for teaching tennis. Here are a few common drills:

1. Mark the Spot: Most kids are so caught up in the right technique they forget about the end result. Where do they want the ball to go? Mark the Spot uses depth perception to create this awareness. After the shot is made and the ball bounces on the opposite court, the player calls out the number of feet from the baseline the ball landed, either long or short. The goal is to see how accurate the estimate is.
2. Height Drill: This is similar to Mark the Spot. In the Height drill, the player calls out number of feet, how far the ball passes over the net cord.

Sighting the Ball

Try this activity with your retriever dog. Grab a tennis ball and draw slow imaginary circles two feet above the dog's face while he sits, first clockwise and then counter-clockwise. Observe his eyes fixated on the ball, tracking its slightest movement. As soon as you throw the ball, within seconds he is able to fetch it for you.

Fido's secret? You guessed it – fast feet and, more importantly, his ability to track the circling ball and spring into action the instant it leaves your hand. The ability to sight the ball as it leaves a competitor's racket will maximize the time a player has to chase down a shot.

Many teaching professionals use the Bounce-Hit set of drills to get kids to focus on the ball from the time the opponent strikes it. In the basic Bounce-Hit drill, each player calls-out "Bounce" when the ball bounces on his side of the court and "Hit" when he makes the shot.

Toss-Hit-Bounce-Hit is a variation suitable for practicing return of serves. As the competitor tosses and hits the serve, the receiving player tracks the ball and calls out "Toss" and "Hit." When the ball lands on his side of the court he calls "Bounce" and finally "Hit" at the time the ball is struck.

Staying Focused

Watch Gustavo "Guga" Kuerten between points. With his trademark wry smile, Guga is a picture of relaxed concentration: adjusting the strings, staring down the lines, and occasionally glancing at his opponent.

For every hour of a tennis match, the ball is in play for less than 15 minutes. The other 45 minutes is "between-the-points" time, changeovers, and time spent retrieving the ball and preparing to serve. It's easy to let the mind wander and get all wound up in the score, that troubling first-serve, or even the ecstatic, "My gosh, I can't believe I'm so far ahead of this great player!" The more distractions, the more difficult it becomes to recover focus when play resumes.

Timothy Gallwey recommends paying attention to breathing in the 25 seconds or so between points. This does not mean controlling breathing. It is simply a technique to bring back the wandering mind and help the player regain focus.

A second suggestion for staying focused between points is offered by sports psychologist Karl Slaikeu and tour pro Robert Trogolo. In their book Focused for Tennis the duo present a mental conditioning system they call the 3 R's:

- ✓ Release negative emotions that come from lost points or dropped games.
- ✓ Review what's happened so far: what's working, what's not.
- ✓ Reset for the next point; bring focus back to the play.

The Other Parent

You can teach your kid all you want but you have to take into account the effect of his "other parent" – the television. Say you just talked to your kid about how effort is more important than winning during the development phase. He then watches a certain television show where little Tommy is the toast of the town because he won the little league championship for the home team. Maybe the show portrayed Tommy working hard, and that's good. But the fact that everyone on the show is completely focused on winning at all costs is not good. It may make for an exciting television episode, but it sends the wrong message, one opposite to what you want to teach.

Media so saturates our lives it isn't possible to protect kids from every message that runs counter to those of parents. Whether the television message is right or wrong, it undoubtedly plays a role in the development of your child's mental attitudes.

Setting good television habits can help. For instance, teach your young child to ask permission to watch television. Take advantage of the new gizmos that let you record the programs you're comfortable allowing your child to watch. Share television shows with positive messages with your child. Always be aware, for better or worse, your messages compete with little Tommy from the Tommy Show for your child's attention.

Drug Abuse

Professional tennis players are tested for recreational drugs and steroids at tournaments, and even outside competition at any time and place requested by the administrators. International Doping Tests and Management (IDTM. More info: idtm.com) is responsible for drug testing and conducts over 1,000 in-competition and 100 out-of-competition drug tests on the men's professional tennis tour alone.

A positive test results in up to a two-year suspension. A second offense can lead to a lifetime ban. The Anti-Doping program for junior competition administered by the USTA is no kinder. How's that for dissuading a young player from ever considering drug abuse?

Avoiding Burnout

If there's only one thing we do to avoid burnout in a young tennis player it must be managing the type and number of tournaments she plays. During the development phase of a young player, rewarding effort and de-emphasizing match results is certainly necessary. But no amount of mental coaching can help a player who is constantly losing in the first round. Before long she will burn out and quit the sport. Conversely, too much winning leads to boredom. A top-ranked teenager can become emotionally spent trying to stay on top, tournament after tournament.

Manage Tournament Play

Adjust the level of competition so the win-loss record over several months is about two wins to each loss. Making it past the second round on a regular basis is one indication that the level of competition is just right to keep the kid motivated. Consider entering both singles and doubles events to achieve the overall win-loss record.

If wins are too high, enter higher-level tournaments. Too many first-round losses? Focus more on skill development and enter lower-level tournaments. With hundreds of regional tournament opportunities for various ages and levels, managing development this way shouldn't be difficult.

Other Passions

Develop a passion for other activities – hobbies and sports. While the kid is into tennis competitively, encourage her to participate in a different sport each season as recreation. Playing a variety of sports also exercises muscles differently and chronic injuries are less likely to occur.

"Children should not only play more than one sport, but also they should cultivate other interests such as computers, music or the arts so they don't always focus on that next tournament," says Michelle Klein, executive director of the National Youth Sports Safety Foundation in Boston.

Take a break from all organized sports for two or three weeks a year. Taking time out, going on vacation, or attending a family reunion will replenish the mind and body. Umm... at least *most* reunions are replenishing.

Have a Higher Goal

Oracene Price-Williams raised her famous daughters to believe that religion and family come before tennis. "Thanks to my God, Jehovah!" Serena Williams exclaimed after winning the French Open and Wimbledon back to back. Religion, community service, and involvement in public causes can help keep tennis in perspective.

Setting priorities will ease needless pressure and may actually benefit your child's game by allowing her to stay relaxed. For example, explain that schoolwork comes first, and then sports.

Detecting Early Signs of Burnout

You have taken all steps necessary to avoid burnout – managed her tournament play, ensured her participation in other activities, and encouraged her to develop goals beyond tennis. How do you know if these are working?

Burnout often kicks in when kids reach their teens. When they're young they generally go along with whatever their parents have planned for them. Meanwhile, years of junior competition and over-scheduling may have taken a secret toll – physically and emotionally. Around adolescence, kids begin to assert themselves more and express their true feelings.

Detect burnout early and make needed changes. According to experts, a child who asks to miss practice, or complains about her coach or the class, is really telling you there's a problem. Often a child suffering from burnout will show signs of sleep disturbance, headache, and muscular rigidity. She may also show signs of depression, such as sadness and lack of energy.

As soon as you are reasonably sure that the problem is burnout, cut back on tennis and extra-curricular activities. If she has been exclusively focused on tennis, encourage participation in another activity. Make that new activity, rather than tennis, the focus of dinner conversation.

Redefine "Making It"

Okay, Mr. Jones, please lay down on the couch and let's talk.

In our hearts, we parents and coaches are conditioned to define "making it" in the world of tennis as winning a Grand Slam. We visualize success in tennis as a pyramid and subconsciously prod our kids and ourselves toward what we believe is the "pinnacle."

Instead of the pyramid, imagine the landscape as a beautiful valley of flowers. Surrounding the valley are gorgeous mountains. You and your kid are enjoying a beautiful hike up the side of one of these mountains. First you conquer one mountain, then another. Anytime you choose you can have a picnic on a rock or in the valley of flowers.

Each mountain presents different challenges. If one is the tallest, the other has the highest rock face; yet another tests navigational skills. In other words, there is no one Mt. Everest in this valley. You can enjoy an "ultimate" challenge by scaling each of them. Or you can choose to simply enjoy the beauty of the trek.

"Okay, okay, Dr. Filbur, I think I got the imagery – not a pyramid but a valley of flowers and mountains and all that. Now you expect me to read this passage to my 10-year-old? You must be kidding, right?"

Actually you don't have to say a word. Just believe in it and live it in your everyday words and actions. Trust me, the kid will soon learn to discover a Mt. Everest in every mountain he climbs. More importantly, whether you and your kid are climbing the mountains or relaxing in the valley of flowers, you will both learn to enjoy today's challenges and rewards.

You may get off the couch now. That will be $125, Mr. Jones. Thank you.

11

Pushing: How much is too much

"I believe you should push your child. Not only is it okay, it is your right, responsibility and your absolute moral imperative as a parent."
DR. JIM TAYLOR, Positive Pushing.

Parents want the best for their children and their goals usually center around helping the child to be confident, happy, and of good character. Why is it then that children, especially adolescents, resist our well-intentioned efforts to help? Why is it that loving parents sometimes feel the need to push – to direct the child to do something they don't want to do? These paradoxes are often most apparent in cases of sports parents.

Parental Goals

Sports psychologists trace many parent-child conflicts to parental goals that are outcome-based and confuse the child's goals with their own. Setting outcome-based goals is tempting and deceptively easy.

"I want to do everything I can to help my 10-year old become the next Andre Agassi." Achieving this so-called "parental" goal is dependent on four actions:

1. The child has to take up tennis, not as a sport but as a career.
2. The child has to put in the necessary practice hours.
3. The parent is able to provide the financial support necessary to reach the goal.
4. The parent is able to provide the time and emotional support necessary to reach the goal.

Clearly, 50 percent of the actions required to accomplish this goal successfully is dependent upon the child. If the child wholeheartedly embraces his end of the deal then everything should be fine. However, there will be trouble in paradise when an adolescent decides to change course to pursue other goals or to divvy up his limited time engaging in other activities. The outcome-based parental goal is suddenly no longer achievable, leaving the parent bewildered and frustrated.

Instead, revise the parental goal to something more specific and directly controllable. For instance, "I will provide the financial help to pursue serious tennis development." Certainly setting such a goal does not preclude a parent from trying to pique the child's interest in tennis or actively encouraging him to take up serious tennis development. The process-based parental goal simply clarifies that the adolescent is the one in the driver's seat, while the parent plays a supportive role as far as tennis development is concerned.

Process-based goals that a tennis parent can set for himself include:

- Highlight the value of tennis as a lifetime sport for fun, fitness, and skill development.
- Provide necessary time and financial and emotional support.
- Use tennis as a vehicle to teach good attitude, teamwork, discipline, and character.

Choose a parental goal that will offer you a sense of accomplishment, whether your child ultimately decides to take up tennis, soccer, law, or medicine.

Why Parents get Pushy?

After years of financially supporting a child's tennis development and carting her to lessons and tournaments, even the most patient parent can be ready to explode. "Jill, win this match or else…" There is no excuse for actually saying such a thing, but it illustrates how parental pressure can fester. Parents feel that because they're contributing time and money, they're also justified in demanding a result – winning.

Measuring Results by Wins

Parents are perfectly justified in demanding results. At the very least, it helps them decide whether their time and money has been well spent. However, the trick is to measure results not by a young child's wins, but by the development of good attitudes and improvements in tennis skill. Parents who measure results this way are less likely to push unjustifiably.

Winning is nice, but winning is only a desirable outcome. The purpose of sport for a child is to create an opportunity for fun and growth. The triumphs and heartaches inherent in sport can provide a child with the learning experiences and life lessons that help pave the road to adulthood.

Ask yourself – Is Jill regularly picking up on important life lessons on the court? Is the game emotionally healthy for her? Has it made her more mature and better prepared for life? If the answer to these questions is yes, your time and money have been well spent, regardless of the outcome of a match.

After a few years of tennis, you can add a second component to monitoring progress – improvements in tennis skills. Sports psychologists say that emphasis on sports mastery demonstrates a focus on performance, whereas emphasis on sports competence is used to describe focus on winning or losing.

Under-emphasis on mastery and over-emphasis on sports competence account for many children appearing to fall short of parental expectations. When that happens, parents intuitively begin to push harder. Instead, measure the results as improvements in skill mastery – better strokes, strategy, physical ability, and mental toughness.

Life lessons and improvements in tennis skills are the yardsticks parents should use to measure results. Chances are, you'll notice your kid has made great progress in vital areas, in spite of losing her match, making all your efforts worthwhile.

Early Parental Goal

Another reason parents are driven to push is that they decide very early on that they are going to raise the child to be a professional tennis player. First, a parent is making a crucial life choice for the child that may not survive her adolescent years. Next, the pressure to constantly practice and perform takes the "sport" out of the game. Instead, it becomes "work" for the child. As a result, the parent has to push even harder to get the child to practice.

Statistically, about 10 to 15 percent of junior competitors earn college scholarships. Less than two percent become professional players. Notwithstanding the statistical long shot, what tennis parent wouldn't want their child to be the next Andre Agassi or Chris Evert? Any parent would be ecstatic to see their kid reach the pinnacle of the game. By all means dream big for your child, but always remember that this is *your* dream, not your child's.

Success at the professional level is more dependent on ability than on effort. Undoubtedly, it takes tremendous effort to maintain a top 100 professional ranking. But what differentiates No. 1 from No. 100 is more ability than effort.

The decision whether to turn professional should really be made based on a scientific method rather than at the emotional level. Periodically, as a child develops and is playing regional and national 14s to 18s tournaments, the parent, the coach, and an athletic trainer, along with the kid, ought to make an honest assessment about whether she has the ability, at all levels, to turn professional.

Understand, the choice to become a professional should be made much later in a child's tennis development and that it is a team decision based on a scientific method. Doing so can help a parent be less pushy.

The trick is to keep the dream of becoming a professional player in perspective; look at it as just one of many equally challenging and ambitious aspirations you have for her. Perhaps, as a parent, you also have hopes that she will one day graduate from an Ivy league college, become a life-saving doctor, a public service lawyer, or head up a volunteer organization that gives back to the community.

And, it bears repeating, always remind yourself that these are *your* dreams and not your child's. Separate your dreams from your parental goals. And remember – you have little control over whether your adolescent child aligns her dreams and goals with yours. It's best to avoid verbalizing your dreams to the child or, as the British would say, "Keep mum." Instead, keep working toward your parental goals.

That the journey is the reward might be a cliché; nevertheless, it is so true. As world-renowned performance psychologist Dr. Jim Loehr so poignantly put it – the value in learning the game of tennis and playing it has to be of the moment, in the present. "If today was the last day my child played tennis, it was still worth it." Repeat this to yourself and you'll find less reason to push.

Sacrifices – Too Many, Too Soon

"You have to understand that nobody in skating realizes, starting out, just how expensive it's going to get," advised World champion figure skater Kristi Yamaguchi's father, Jim, in the San Jose Mercury News. "It sort of creeps up on you, because as Kristi got better, she began to have more needs, so we got in deeper and deeper."

Commitment to tennis is no different, and possibly even more expensive. A tennis career will require that the family make choices and compromises: missed social activities with family and friends; educational and career plans postponed; houses in different states –

one for the working parent and the other where the care-taking parent lives with the child – a necessity for better coaching and competitive opportunities.

Reasonable compromises are okay, but only after a decision has been made to take up tennis as a career. "Parents can say we love you no matter what, and just do your best – all the right things," says psychologist Stan Ziegler, quoted in Tennis magazine. But if the family then organizes its life around the kid's pursuit of a professional career, it doesn't matter what you say. The kid still thinks, "Jeez, my whole family is depending on me."

Sometimes parents make sacrifices very early on, when the child has just started playing tennis simply as recreation and there is no evidence yet of consistent performance or ability. And, most importantly, before the child has developed the maturity to weigh in on whether to take up tennis as a career.

Hard sacrifices, especially financial ones, made too early in a child's training add to the child's mental burden. Juniors confess to having to work hard to block out thoughts of their family's financial and lifestyle sacrifices during a match. And, at some level, tennis development suffers. Once families invest so much of themselves in tennis, it clouds decision-making. Children find it harder to quit if they want to.

We like to believe that anything is possible, but parents ought to look ahead to the financial demands of competitive sport. This doesn't mean you can't help your child succeed even if income is limited. A little planning goes a long way. Trade off a few private lessons for self-practice; buy cheaper equipment or travel to fewer competitions and, when you do go, stay at inexpensive hotels.

Planning ahead for the financial commitments will ease pressure on the parent. A parent not consumed with money worries is less likely to be pushy, thus creating a healthier and more relaxed environment for the child's tennis development.

Some parents wisely limit the amount of money and time they're prepared to invest. In 1990, when Chanda Rubin was 14, she became the youngest player selected for the USTA national team. Yet she managed to accomplish this without the heavy investment in training most young tennis players make.

Rubin's tennis instruction was limited to group lessons three times a week at a club near her home. Not until three weeks before her first US Open did she switch to more expensive private lessons.

Today, Rubin has earned a career-high sixth ranking in the world and amassed more than a dozen WTA titles.

Playing Up

Opting to "play up" – the practice of competing in an older age division – can be quite an ego-trip for the parent. The decision to play-up a mature and competitive kid who is consistently trouncing his peers is cut and dried. To keep him challenged and interested, have him compete in an older age division tournament.

In the case of a younger child, the decision needs more careful consideration. A 9-year-old may be consistently outplaying his peers, but you have to consider that he's also having a lot of fun practicing with them. Maybe the kids have formed an adventure club and play together regularly after tennis practice. Moving the kid to an older age group could be great for his tennis, but may not appeal to him socially.

Another pitfall to watch out for is when a young child who is playing up begins to develop a convenient excuse for losing. Parents may also have a tendency to convince themselves the child is losing because his competitors are older. Such rationalizations can prevent kids from developing mental toughness.

Experts suggest that the best way to take advantage of the benefits of playing up, while avoiding the drawbacks, is to "mix it up." For younger children who are consistently outperforming their age group, start by phasing in practice sessions with the next older group. A kid practicing three times a week can be allowed to practice with the older group once a week, while continuing to practice with his peers.

In these instances, a wise coach will try to avoid creating the impression that one particular kid is being handpicked for promotion. In some cases, kids who are playing up may need to return to their own age group. They may not enjoy the new challenge or perhaps the coach will decide the kid is not quite ready. This can feel like a demotion to the child. Consider playing up as a part of the regular program and do it without a lot of hoopla.

When the kid develops consistency in the older age group and is able to win some practice games, he is ready to be phased in to a similar tournament schedule. A proficient 9-year old can pick high-level tournaments in his age group – the 10s. Mix things up by adding two or three rookie tournaments in the 12s age group.

After six months, if his win-loss ratio is 2 or 3 to 1 or better, ante-up the level of tournaments in the older age group. Instead of rookie tournaments in the 12s age group, substitute two or three higher-level tournaments. Very rarely should kids be allowed to play up more than a single age group.

Kids develop faster when they play with older children. Playing up is necessary to keep proficient kids engaged, but it is still best to mix in play in their age group so they continue to have fun and develop a social network at practice and at tournaments.

Played Out

Greg Moran and his wife are teaching pros at a family-owned tennis club. Greg's father is a former Davis Cup star. When Greg started his two kids on tennis lessons, he believed they had many factors going for them – a favorable gene pool, teaching pros in the family, and a year-round tennis facility.

The Morans were very careful to avoid the pitfalls of the "tennis parent syndrome." They were not interested in raising tennis champions; they simply wanted to give their children a chance to enjoy the sport for the rest of their lives, just as their parents had passed a love of tennis on to them.

They started the kids early with lessons and took them out for the occasional family hitting session, always attempting to keep it light and fun. Then a funny thing happened: the kids told them they didn't like tennis.

The parents listened and, though they told the kids they would never force them to stick with an activity they didn't like, they urged them to give it another try. The kids agreed but, eventually, comments like "tennis is stupid" and "I hate tennis" began creeping into their conversation.

The case of another tennis parent is even more dramatic. For years Kathy shuttled her son to and from practice and spent thousands of dollars on lessons. Her son was doing well, entering dozens of tournaments, and earning a top 20 sectional ranking. But by the time he was 12, the boy was ready to quit tennis.

The stories of Kathy and the Morans are by no means isolated instances. Kids quit tennis for lots of reasons. In the case of the Moran children, they viewed tennis as "work" because it's what their parents do for a living.

For Kathy's son, who enjoyed early success, his peers were catching up with him and this rattled his confidence. He became afraid to play a sport in which he could be beaten by kids he'd regularly trounced years before.

Prevention

Specific strategies can be employed by parents and coaches to help prevent the "I want to quit" syndrome before the fact.

- Avoid pushing young kids into a high degree of specialization in a single sport.
- Many parents believe coaching their child strains the parent-child relationship. Leave the coaching to a professional.
- Emphasize sports mastery over competence. Teach kids to enjoy the process of developing proficiency. Help them measure accomplishments by improvement in various skills rather than whom they beat or lost to. "My breakpoint conversion rose to 40 percent today" is a better yardstick for junior competitors than "Today, I beat Sally."
- Enter tournaments that allow the child to sustain a win-loss ratio of 2 or 3 to 1.
- Be prepared to lessen the degree of parental involvement in decision-making as the child grows older.

Now What?

A parent has done all the right things, yet sometimes the kid is ready to quit anyway. Sports psychologists say up until ages 10 to 12, a child will probably go along with what Dad and Mom suggest. Over the next couple of years, though, the child wants to begin making her own decisions, including those related to sports participation. By adolescence, the influence of peers is replacing that of parents.

Leaving tennis behind might be the kid's way of asserting independence. "Mom and Dad want me to play, so I won't." Or maybe it's time to face the fact that they really don't like the game. Whatever the reason, parents ought to prepare for the day when their child announces, "I want to quit tennis," whether that day actually arrives or not.

Remember, the choice to play should always be the child's. All you can do is gently nudge them in the direction that you believe is best for them. Let's say your young child has expressed some interest in tennis. You think she might enjoy it and let her sign up for tennis lessons. Three weeks into the lessons, she hates them. "All I do is chase the ball," she complains.

At that point, the best choice is to make her stick with it. Often, after a few lessons, the child becomes more proficient and may want to continue. Younger children may be confused about the rules of the game. Explain the rules or practice with them so they feel more comfortable. In any case, she only has a few weeks to go and she'll probably learn a valuable lesson by following through on something she started but now doesn't enjoy. Be sympathetic, but firm. Don't force her to sign up for the next program, but make her finish this one.

Older children may have more complex reasons for wanting to quit. Help your child articulate those reasons. Talk to her coach. Study her performance at practice sessions and tournaments. Think about whether one or more of the following come into play.

1. Tennis isn't fun anymore: Make sure the coach is compatible with your child. Tread carefully, but don't be afraid to try a new coach. Maybe your child has been played up too quickly and is unable to keep up, preventing her from having fun. Reduce competitions; instead, focus on casual practice with family and friends. Rekindle interest by taking her to watch a professional or regional tournament. Sometimes simply taking a complete break from tennis for two to three weeks can help the child return with enthusiasm.
2. Too much pressure: A kid can experience pressure from a parent, coach, or teammates. Maybe it's time for the parent to get out of the advice business and leave the training to the coach. Praise effort, skills, and technique rather than focusing on bottom-line wins and losses. Maybe the school team needs opportunities to bond and relax outside of tennis. Find time to play tennis with the family. Replace a weekly hour of tennis with another hobby – music, photography, or anything else you know interests your child.
3. Not enough time: Experts recommend focusing on one extra-curricular activity at a time. Help your child prioritize. Instead of doing both soccer and tennis each week, suggest she select one sport and put off learning the other until there's an opportunity to attend a related sports camp. Of course, as a loyal tennis parent, you will instinctively guide her toward tennis as a first choice, won't you? Don't worry, these things have a way of sorting themselves out.
4. Mismatched skill level: Again, this means the child has cither been played up too quickly or placed in an inappropriate class where her skill level doesn't match that of others in her group. Perhaps not enough attention has been paid to learning the basics. Go back to the drawing board. A few months of private lessons and a different class level may be just what the doctor ordered.

Sometimes, though, even these methods don't work. It's not uncommon for children between the ages of 12 and 14 to lose interest in a sport. Rick Wolff, a well-known sports psychologist, says this is not always due to burnout. The child may simply have more of an affinity for another activity and wants to budget precious hours towards that activity. While it is okay to stop pursuing a sport, ensure that the child puts time and energy into another productive outlet.

If every tennis lesson counts as a life lesson, then nothing has been lost. Remember that. Once you've exhausted all strategies and your child comes to you to announce, once and for all, that she's joining the band instead of her high school tennis team, train yourself to respond as Greg Moran did: "Do your best kid, and have fun."

Key Parental Roles

Few players have reached their potential without support from their families. This support can be expressed in many ways – love, money, guidance, motivation, coaching, time, and travel assistance. There are other parental roles that may not be as obvious but, nonetheless, determine whether a child becomes not just a tennis player, but a healthy young adult.

Parental Involvement: Finding a balance

We hear stories of famous parents like Richard and Oracene Price-Williams, who make major contributions to their children's development by staying involved. Generally, a parent's involvement ought to focus on financial and emotional support, character development, and education.

Having carefully chosen a coach, a parent should let the coach and junior player decide on lessons, practice, and competition structure. Periodic conferences with the coach and child will help communicate parental goals, assess progress, and synchronize tournament travel with family plans. In the 6 to 12 age group, the time when experts suggest it's okay for a trained, tennis-proficient parent to coach, one consideration ought to dominate everything else, and that's keeping the game fun.

Sometimes parents get over-involved, scrutinizing every practice and agonizing over each loss. The trick is keeping the outcome in perspective. When the primary reason for parental involvement in a child's tennis is to teach goal setting, discipline, and increasing self-esteem, a parent can't go wrong.

Physical Fitness

Physical conditioning is too often an after thought, even though any professional will tell you how central proper conditioning is to junior development. As the coach essentially works on the kid's tennis, it's up to the parent to help carry out conditioning routines.

Parental support can be a determining factor in whether a tennis kid stays healthy, fit, and injury-free. Parents have to insist on proper warm-up and stretches, before and after practice. They may have to arrive a little early for a lesson so the kid can get in an effective warm up.

The weekly workout doesn't have to be "work." Fun routines such as medicine balls, hula loops, skipping rope, playing basketball on the driveway, or walking the dog are creative ways to get the child conditioned. It helps when parents lead active lifestyles, too.

Encourage Your Child to Dream

Goal setting is about keeping feet planted firmly on the ground and choosing goals over which one has a reasonable degree of control. Children, however, are natural dreamers. The movie October Sky is the triumphant true story of Homer Hickam, Jr., a high school student in 50s rural West Virginia who refuses to give up his dream, regardless of how unrealistic it seems to the adults in his life.

Too small to earn a football scholarship, Homer is destined to follow in his father footsteps and become a coal miner. Until the Soviets challenge America with the successful launch of the Sputnik satellite, that is. With the help of his loyal band of friends, Homer embarks on a mission to build and launch his own homemade rocket.

Despite repeated setbacks and early failures that nearly get them shut down, the group of friends stick with it and do the impossible, successfully launching a functional rocket and winning prestigious college scholarships in the process. Their success inspires the whole town to believe miracles can happen, even in Coalwood, and that there's nothing wrong with shooting for the stars.

Children's dreams are the stuff of creativity; they are the fuel that motivates them to try the impossible. Dr. Alan Goldberg, a nationally known expert in sports psychology, advises parents to encourage children to dream. Inspire them. Tell them stories of all the "impossible" things that have been accomplished by people following their dreams.

Help the child understand the difference between goal setting and dreaming. For instance, developing a consistent first-serve percentage of 75 percent is an ambitious goal, but if one practices smart and hard, there is a good chance of accomplishing it. On the other hand, beating the No.1 ranked player in the world might be considered a dream because it presents too many variables outside one's control. For instance, one can't control how hard the No. 1 player practices.

By all means, encourage your child to dream big and chase his dreams, to set big goals and go after them. But also teach your child to measure success by goals accomplished rather than dreams realized. This is the practical way they learn to relish the process and lead successful lives, even though not all dreams come true.

Keep 'em Playing

Watching a group of tennis kids play and grow together over the years is a fascinating study in physical and psychological development. One day you see them as 8-year olds, playing and behaving similarly. Come back after the holiday season and at least one of the boys has probably shot up in height. His tennis ability is now likely to be above everyone else in the class, too.

Give it a season or two; a couple of the girls have not only caught up with the boy in height, but some will be starting to overtake him. Their tennis ability may well follow. A child's tennis development occurs in sporadic spurts, even past the adolescent stage.

The key is to keep them interested in tennis whether you think they have the ability needed for the sport at that time or not. More importantly, even if the child feels she lacks natural talent, encourage her to persist. When she catches the next growth spurt, she is bound to do better and her interest level will bounce back.

Basketball legend Michael Jordan did not make his high school team, even as a sophomore, because he just wasn't good enough at the time. A kid who is so-so at 10 years old may be a kid who is great at 16, and vice versa. It's a shame for a kid to drop out before he can find out how good he can be. Conversely, a kid used to dominating at an early age may drop out at 16 because he can no longer do so.

The best thing a parent and coach can do is to encourage tennis mastery over winning or losing. Competing with one's own ability naturally discourages unnecessary comparison with other kids during the growth phase. Physical changes, especially in girls, can lead to uneven performance on some days. Gently nudge kids through the ups and downs of tennis. With the growth spurts one never knows who'll turn out to be the super player.

The Reserve Parachute

Life has a perverse way of throwing curve balls – injury, burnout, an unexpected move, financial fallout. Some parents feel they ought to help develop another talent, in case the child is unable to pursue his interest in tennis, or at least pursue it as seriously as he wants to. Like a skydiver using dual parachutes, a child should be encouraged early on to pursue other interests, not as much for backup as for a more rounded childhood development.

All tennis, all the time can become exhausting. A second passion offers an outlet to break away from the intensity of tennis for a while and return rejuvenated. Jim Courier, the French Open champion, got his first drum set when he was 3 years old. His first racket came later. After his retirement from tennis, Courier traded in his racket for his third love – a guitar.

Positive Pushing

The argument for pushing is really simple. Kids love any activity they're good at. Becoming good requires practice. As long as practice is fun, kids will do it. This is the "high" of the sport. Sometimes, though, they may need to practice skills that are a little hard to learn. A two-handed backhander may need a gentle push to help the child sustain an effort to learn the one-handed backhand. It's during these times – the "lows" of tennis – that a parent has to push.

The bottom-line is, for healthy development of a tennis kid the highs have to outweigh the lows. When it becomes necessary to push a child through the lows, the parent or coach has to do so in a way that is deliberate and vigorous, but always with a positive message that reaffirms your unconditional love and helps to build self-esteem.

Dr. Jim Taylor is a psychologist who lived the life of a young achiever. A top-ranked skier, certified tennis coach, black belt in karate, marathon runner, and an Ironman triathlete, he has developed five tips for "positive pushing":

1. Set expectations that emphasize healthy values that will help your child become successful and happy. For example, focus on hard work,

responsibility, cooperation, patience and persistence, rather than expectations that stress grades, results and other outcomes.
2. Allow your child to experience all emotions, don't assuage, placate or distract them from their feelings. Help them to identify, understand and express their emotions in a healthy way.
3. Actively manage the child's environment and activities – peer interactions, achievement activities, cultural experiences, leisure pursuits – in ways that reflect the values, attitudes and behaviors that you want the child to adopt.
4. Create options from which a child can choose a direction. Stress that doing nothing is not an option.
5. Help your child find something they love and are passionate about in their efforts. They will be successful and happy.

Achieving success in almost anything requires a sustained effort that will always have its highs – the fun parts, and lows – the parts one doesn't like to do. The trick is to maximize the highs and ride out the lows through positive pushing.

12

Money Wise

"Don't worry about money. If we do the right things, there will always be plenty of money."
ROBERT KIYOSAKI, Rich Dad's Guide To Investing.

What's nice about tennis is that the cost of recreational play can be virtually zilch. Once you own the initial equipment – a box of balls and a racket, both of which are easily affordable – hitting all day at a public court costs nothing. It doesn't take a whole lot of time and money to learn the game either. A week of introductory lessons at a summer camp, or an eight-week program of weekly group classes is all a kid needs to pick up the basic strokes.

The Cost of Raising a Tennis Kid

As a kid begins to show serious interest in developing his game, a little initial budgeting goes a long way. However, earning a ranking at the regional and national levels takes serious bucks. Parents report an annual outlay for the serious junior player ranging from $15,000 to $50,000, depending upon how far away the major tournaments are held and the intensity of coaching.

A Sample Estimate

At the higher echelons of junior competition the real kicker is the tournament expense. That includes travel for the player and his entourage – a parent or coach – and accommodations. Private lessons, group clinics, and camps are a close second, expense wise.

Table 12.1 gives a sample estimate of costs to train a junior player over an eight-year period. Year 1 is when the junior decides to move from recreational play to serious tennis development. Estimates for Years 7 and 8 include costs associated with high-performance training and national and international travel.

Instead of hassling with the logistical details of travel and coaching, some parents choose to enroll the child in a tennis academy.

Table 12.1

Year	Level	Equipment Includes rackets, shoes, balls, and attire.	Coaching Includes lessons, tournament training, and camps.	Competition Includes travel, hotel, and entry fees.	Total
1	Novice	$375	$1,670		$2,045
2	Regular	$520	$1,990	$240	$2,750
3	Regular	$555	$1,990	$300	$2,845
4	Sectional	$555	$2,240	$1,080	$3,875
5	Regional	$825	$3,060	$2,460	$6,345
6	Regional	$825	$3,060	$2,460	$6,345
7	National	$825	$7,280	$8,650	$16,755
8	National	$825	$9,280	$9,350	$19,455

In addition to tennis instruction and tournament travel, an elite tennis academy takes care of physical and mental conditioning, high-performance coaching, room and board, and a regular academic education. The all-inclusive package can set you back upwards of $70,000 annually.

The Good News

If your jaw is beginning to drop, lock it back into place – there's good news. The USTA, mandated to "grow the game," is trying to put more American players at the top rungs of the competitive ladder. One way it hopes to do that is by offering grants for player development. The parents of a top junior can often cut their bills by 20 percent or more with these grants.

Individual and corporate enterprise also play a big part in developing players by offering scholarships and sponsorships. A few months after Andre Agassi entered the Bollettieri Tennis Academy, Nick Bollettieri offered young Andre a full scholarship. Rick Macci saw great potential after watching 11-year-old Venus Williams practice on the courts of her rough neighborhood in Compton, California. Macci subsequently offered to subsidize coaching, relocated the Williams sisters to Delray Beach, Florida, and helped them earn a corporate sponsorship.

It is not only the famous coaches who help out financially. Many local teaching professionals, bless their hearts, subsidize their fees, on a case-by-case basis, for promising juniors who cannot otherwise afford the lessons.

Tennis equipment manufacturers like Wilson, Nike, Prince, and Reebok make a significant contribution to player development by offering free rackets, clothing, and other support to top-ranked juniors who are competing at the sectional and national levels.

In the early years of tennis development, the costs are more or less the same as they are in other sports. However, as the player gets into serious tennis competition at the sectional and national levels, the bucks can add up fast. So, it is gratifying to know there are many individuals and organizations willing to chip in at that level of competition. Combine this with some smart planning and savvy saving tips and any parent should be able to see their tennis kid through serious competition.

On the Cheap

The wholesale shipment of sporting goods tops $49 billion annually, according to the Sporting Goods Manufacturers Association. That includes sports and fitness equipment, athletic footwear, and sports apparel. It's not hard to find the reason for this astonishing sales total. Just check out the price tag on the Kournikova look-alike attire your little angel wants so badly.

If you don't have money to burn on the extras: designer attire, expensive equipment, brand name lessons, and costly accommodations – take heart. With a little creativity you can limit the costs and stay within your means. Being money wise can also teach your child an important life lesson.

Rackets

Whatever else you skimp on, experts will tell you not to skimp on rackets. An ill-suited racket can cause long-term injuries, but you don't have to splurge on high-ticket rackets either.

Quality models are available in the mid-price range. They don't break the bank and are perfect for a child's growing years when children go through one or two rackets each year. You can often find great buys at general merchandise stores and used sports equipment stores like Play It Again Sports. These rackets will be fine for kids who are just getting started in tennis.

Local pro shops and online tennis stores sell closeout models and blemished or slightly used demo rackets at bargain prices. They're worth checking out. You can also visit online auction sites, especially if you know which racket model you want to buy.

Another smart way to save is to turn necessities into presents. Buy your aspiring Venus Williams a new tennis racket for her birthday.

Consider donating old rackets in good condition to charity. Besides warming your heart, donations allow you to save some green on taxes.

Balls

The balls used in tournaments are pressurized. Once a ball can is opened, air seeps out and the balls lose their bounce. A pressurized ball typically lasts three to six sets of match play, or three hours of practice play. After the can is opened, stored balls lose bounce in three to five weeks. The best tip to stretch your budget is to choose the most durable balls. Try different brands and determine which balls last the longest for your type of use.

✓ *Ball Pressurizer*: Consider using a ball pressurizer designed to apply the same pressure as the original sealed can. The cost of a ball pressurizer is about $10 and will maintain the life of stored balls. A pressure cap serves the same purpose and costs about the same, too. Instead of a separate pressurizer can, the pressure cap replaces the lid on any standard can of tennis balls.

✓ *Proper storage*: Whether you choose pressurizers or not, avoid leaving used balls in a hot car. Not the red "hot" sporty convertible kind of hot, but the kind even a family minivan becomes when parked under the Florida sun. Return partially used balls to a cool place, which will extend their life.

✓ *Permanent Pressure Balls*: The main problem with regular pressurized balls is that they can get soft and lose their pressure within weeks. Ball machines hold up to 200 balls. Replacing that number of balls every month can be expensive. The permanent-pressure practice ball is a good option. A bucket of balls can last one to two years when used in a ball machine or teaching cart. The permanent-pressure balls are slightly pricier than regular pressurized balls, but their longer life more than makes up for the initial difference in price.

Court Time

If you're paying for court-time or a club membership, you can save yourself a bundle by paying the annual dues in one lump sum. Use public courts whenever possible. They're usually available for unlimited use, as long as no one else is waiting, and they cost nothing.

Lessons

Cut lesson cost in half by signing up for semi-private lessons instead of private ones. By pairing with another student in a semi-private setting, you not only save money, the child is likely to have more fun when he has another kid his age to learn and practice with. Besides, a full hour of one-on-one learning may be too much for a young child to handle. If your child is currently doing half-hour private lessons, consider switching to a one-hour, semi-private format that includes another kid.

Tournament Travel

Take advantage of the hotel discount deals most tournaments offer. Tournaments may also offer private housing. Staying with a local family is a big cost-cutter in tournament travel. Host families are generally carefully screened, but it's a good idea to verify this with the tournament director.

Parents often develop friendships with parents of tennis children from other cities and host each other's kids. Join the frequent-flier and frequent-traveler programs offered by airlines and hotels. Tournament travel is an easy way to rack up additional points. Cash in the earned points for free hotel stays, air travel, and upgrades.

Savings on Stuff

Shoe companies like K-Swiss and many retail stores offer deep discounts on shoes and attire for school and recreational teams. Most tennis suppliers include a free annual supply of shoes, rackets, and attire to top-ranked juniors in their promotional budgets.

The Lemonade Stand

Sidewalk lemonade stands are a cherished memory of childhood. This American rite of passage embodies hard work, dedication, and reward. Once upon a time, the only regulation for lemonade stands was that you had to be home for dinner by six.

Today, Baby Boomers may lament the fact that this simple childhood enterprise now seems to require licenses, liability insurance, and permission from three different government agencies. But watch 8-year-old Anna assist the tennis pro by retrieving all the balls that float outside the court fence. Anna has negotiated a 50 percent discount in her clinic fee for helping the pro during his other clinics. The "lemonade stand" lives on.

An enterprising junior can find many opportunities to save on tennis training and earn pocket change at the same time. As a youngster, Richard "Pancho" Gonzalez, the maverick tennis legend of the 1940s, walked to the nearby high school to watch the tennis team practice. There he made friends with a player named Charles Pate. Soon Richard was helping Pate on his morning newspaper route. In exchange, Pate gave Richard tennis lessons.

A 14- to 18-year-old advanced junior can assist with a tiny-tots class, sweep up a public court for the pro's use, or recycle used tennis balls into dog toys. She can work at the local tennis club in return for court-time, free stringing, or discounted lessons.

If junior's rackets need a lot of re-stringing, consider investing in an adequate stringing machine for under $200. It will pay for itself in no time and junior can make some extra income stringing for other players.

USTA Grants and Scholarships

The USTA offers promising juniors the opportunity to earn grants and scholarships to cover a portion of their expenses for training and travel, camp and education. Selection for the Junior Competition Awards are based on ranking and financial need. There are other awards, like the USA Tennis & Education Foundation scholarships, that go to deserving players, recreational or competitive, based purely on need.

Junior Competition Awards

You can find out about availability and selection criteria by contacting the USTA section office or your local community tennis association (More info: usta.com). Selection is generally determined by age, interest in tennis, good sportsmanship, and financial need.

Each season, Competition Training Centers are used to train a select group of the top-20 players between the ages of 12 and 14 within a given geographical area. In all, over 100 training centers are in place across the United States, providing instruction in the sports sciences and opportunities for drills and match play with other top juniors in the area.

Graduates of the Competition Training Centers are often selected to participate in cross-sectional camps and in training sessions at a Regional Training Center. Typically, the USTA partially covers training and travel expenses.

Top juniors who make the USTA National Team receive training, sports sciences testing, travel and tournament expenses wholly arranged and underwritten by the USTA.

Top-ranked juniors will generally be contacted by the USTA with information about their eligibility for player development training and camps. If that's not the case for your junior, either because she is a beginner or her performance is not yet on the USTA radar screen, contact your local community tennis association and USTA section (More info: usta.com). Tell them about your child's record and current needs and find out whether she's eligible to apply for appropriate grants and scholarships.

USA Tennis & Education Foundation Awards

The USA Tennis & Education Foundation is the charitable and philanthropic arm of the USTA (More info: usta.com). Each year the Foundation awards hundreds of scholarships to deserving youngsters who have participated in USTA youth tennis programs.

The Scholarship Incentive Awards are available to qualified high school varsity players and potential middle school varsity players, while other scholarships go to high school seniors applying for their first year at university.

Private Scholarships

In addition to financial help, a local office of the USTA may be able to point you to other tennis-related philanthropic organizations. The PTR Foundation (More info: ptrtennis.org), Venus and Serena Williams Tennis Academy (More info: venusserenatennisacademy.org), Tenacity (More info: tenacity.org), and Youth Tennis Advantage (More info: youthtennis.org) are a few of the scores of tennis organizations reaching out to the under-privileged.

Finding Sponsorships

You, the consumer, watch a television commercial touting the superiority of Wilson rackets. There's fair chance your next racket purchase will be a Wilson. Now you watch the television coverage of Venus Williams winning a prestigious WTA tournament. The Wilson logo prominently painted on her racket strings is hard to miss. The odds that your next racket purchase will be a Wilson, are now even greater. This is the basic premise for corporate sponsorships.

Corporate Sponsorships

Almost all sporting goods manufacturers, and many other companies, allocate marketing dollars for athlete sponsorships. While the big bucks go to one or two famous athletes, a good portion of the budget is allocated for distribution among a number of up and coming juniors.

A top junior tennis player is no match for Venus Williams on the fame index, but there are good reasons why Wilson or Reebok would want to sponsor a young, relatively unknown player:

- Parents and players hoping to defray training costs are attracted to a sport that offers corporate sponsorships. A sport's popularity moves the company's products.
- Junior tournaments are great testing grounds for consumer opinion.
- By supporting a particular junior, the company is essentially betting she will emerge as a top professional player and become famous. The company wants to earn the goodwill of and develop a relationship with that junior and her parents.

Private Sponsorships

Support from a grandparent, other extended family member, or a community group is a quick way to cover a large, one-time expense such as travel to an important international tournament. If the financial support comes from family members, it's probably best to keep the amounts reasonable so you and your child don't end up feeling uncomfortable about accepting help.

Some companies have a special fund for community outreach programs and may be willing to use some of that to help out employees and their children. There's no guarantee that a company will contribute, but a parent shouldn't automatically assume it won't either. It never hurts to ask.

Individual sponsors, sports marketing companies, player agents, and some tennis academies regularly scout prestigious tournaments hoping to find top talent for sponsorship deals. The Orange Bowl in Key Biscayne, Florida is one such national tournament.

Levels of Sponsorship

The different ways in which a sponsor can support a promising junior are narrowly defined and limited to underwriting a portion of the training, travel, and living expenses. These types of support allow a player to maintain amateur status, making her eligible to apply for college tennis scholarships. Later, should she choose to turn professional, the sponsorship deals can include salaries and signing bonuses.

In general terms, a top player can expect sponsor participation to keep pace with the level of tennis development:

Table 12.2

Level	Type of Sponsorship and Support	Status
Sectional ranking	Discounts on equipment and apparel.	Amateur
Top sectional ranking	Free equipment and apparel; USTA section-level grants for training and travel; college athletic scholarship.	Amateur
Top national ranking	Free equipment and apparel; USTA national-level grants for training and travel; college athletic scholarship.	Amateur
New professional ranking	Free equipment and apparel; support for training and travel; bonuses and contingencies.	Professional
Top professional ranking	Free equipment and apparel; endorsement contracts including salaries, bonuses, and contingencies.	Professional

Keep in mind the level of tennis development and whether or not maintaining amateur status is important when tailoring a sponsorship proposal.

Amateur Status and Athletic Scholarships

Bill Baker, a tennis parent, expresses the predicament of the tennis parent having to choose between amateur and professional status for the child. Baker says in Tennis magazine, "The Babolat Company just called to ask if my daughter, Ally, would shoot a commercial with Andy Roddick. How could I say no to that? I had to check with the NCAA, though, and they OK'd it as long as we don't take any money, or Ally might lose her eligibility for a college scholarship. It's a tough line to walk – a free ride worth $200,000 at a top school is hard to push aside."

Generally speaking, to maintain amateur status, sponsorship money or support should directly underwrite an athlete's training and travel expenses, their being no out-of-the-ordinary quid pro quo agreement. For example, an agreement that purports to fund a player's training for two years, but expects the player to do a photo shoot for the company may be jeopardizing the player's amateur status.

If the player is banking on a college athletic scholarship, it's prudent to check with the NCAA (More info: ncaa.org) before accepting sponsorship support. Of course, amateur status is not necessarily the Holy Grail. When sponsorship money is lucrative and the player doesn't need the scholarship, she can accept sponsorship – effectively turning professional.

Developing a Sponsorship Proposal

Chances are, private sponsors will approach the junior with various levels of sponsorship once she earns a top ranking. For example, at the basic level, sporting goods manufacturers routinely send out free or discount equipment offers to the top-100 or 50 ranked players in each 12s to 18s category each year. The number of offers varies based upon the region, or what the manufacturers refer to as the "tennis market."

If your junior has not been contacted, either because she's a beginner or her performance has not yet been noticed, take heart. There's nothing in the Constitution that says you can't contact potential sponsors yourself.

Before contacting a company, sporting goods manufacturer, or other private sponsor develop a sponsorship proposal. Highlight the player's record and include answers to the following:

- Why do you need a sponsor? Of course you need financial and equipment support. But explain how the support is going to make a difference in training and development.
- How long will you require sponsorship? Is this is a one-time deal or are you looking for multi-year support?
- How much do you need? Be honest about your needs – coaching, equipment and apparel, pre-competition training, travel, and entry fees.
- What do you have to offer a sponsor? Some individual sponsors are altruistic and expect nothing in return. The sporting goods manufacturers that offer free or discounted equipment do it to generate goodwill and don't expect a quid pro quo. But most private sponsors will expect something in return and want to know from your proposal how their sponsorship of your junior will contribute to the company's goals.

In most companies the marketing or promotions department is the contact for sponsorship proposals. Your coach may also be able to identify the local representative of a sporting goods manufacturer who will receive your proposal.

Due Diligence

It's exciting to earn a sponsorship. Unless it's a routine offer – a USTA grant or free or discounted equipment and apparel – the parent should carefully scrutinize the deal and get expert advice from USTA Player Development (More info: usta.com), the NCAA (More info: ncaa.org), and an attorney in order to evaluate the sponsorship. You'll want to know the following:

- The background of the individual sponsor or agent and his reliability going forward.
- The effect of the agreement on planned college scholarships and junior competition.
- What the sponsor will expect from the player.
- The import of contingency clauses and other fine print.

Before signing on the dotted line, consider the player's needs and capabilities and reconfirm that the sponsorship deal helps to meet them.

Internship

Phil de Piccioto, current president of the leading sports marketing company, Octagon, was once an intern at the company. If you're thinking that this dream career path of intern to company president is rare, think again. Alastair Johnston, head of the golf division at the world's largest sports marketing organization, IMG, and the person credited with the financial success of Tiger Woods, also got his start as an intern at IMG.

Most sports business internships pay less than a summer job and some just cover out-of-pocket expenses. But landing an internship at a top sports company can be key for a young tennis player and will help him to appreciate the business side of the sports world, while gaining valuable work experience for future career options.

Many of the large corporations advertise internship opportunities, but most smaller companies don't, simply because no one has asked them for a position. Put them on your call list; they may be thrilled to offer a position. There are all kinds of sports-related internships out there. Here are a just few examples:

- Sports marketing: IMG (More info: imgworld.com), Octagon (More info: octagon.com)
- Sports media: CNN (More info: cnn.com).
- Endorsement businesses: Burns Sports Celebrity Service (More info: burnssports.com).
- Sports related non-profits: Women's Sports Foundation (More info: womenssportsfoundation.org).
- Tennis organizations: USTA (More info: usta.com).
- Summer camps: Start with online directories (More info: shawguides.com and juniortennis.com) and local community centers.
- Teaching professionals: Contact a local professional (More info: uspta.com and ptrtennis.org) to find out about assistantship opportunities.

Large corporations generally seek out applicants at colleges. The ratio of open positions to applicants can be as high as 1 to 20, or more. Local and smaller sized businesses, camps, community centers, and local teaching professionals are the best bet for high school students. Who's to say that summer gig won't turn into a high-flying career?

Publicity for Your Junior

Who wouldn't enjoy reading glowing newspaper articles about themselves? Media coverage that highlights a young player's efforts and accomplishments can be exciting. As long as the coverage doesn't turn the kid into a prima donna, publicity can provide healthy motivation, attract potential sponsors, and inspire other kids.

Make it Unique

Media experts advise potential publicity seekers to look for something unique in their story. There are probably lots of young, aspiring players in many different sports in your area. What's special about your youngster's story? Often times, it's simply a matter of good timing. A local affiliate of the NBC television network aired a tennis segment about 6 and 10-year-old African American sisters from the area. The reason? Venus and Serena Williams were playing in a WTA event in the same region.

Talking of the Williams sisters, how did siblings playing on the dusty courts of Compton get the attention of top coaches and potential sponsors on the opposite coast? Top performance is one reason. Between the ages of 9 and 11, Venus compiled a stunning 63-0 record. Well-placed publicity is another reason. Tennis magazine ran its first article about her in 1991. Richard Williams has never been shy about telling reporters how his kids broke through traditional barriers with hard work and the right attitude.

Tools of the Trade

Establish direct contact with journalists. Before that, assemble the communication tools you will need:

- Targeted media list: Names, email addresses, phone and fax numbers of reporters who cover sports and youth-related stories. Newspapers, magazines, television and radio stations, and web sites are the media outlets you should consider contacting.
- Prepare a media kit: Information about the player's record and planned activities; points you would like highlighted, photographs, and third-party quotes.

• Identify a spokesperson: Designate a parent, coach, or relative as the exclusive contact for the media.

Create your own buzz. Develop interesting story angles and pitch them to the media on an ongoing basis.

Homeschooling

This may remind you of your ACT and SAT tests. Homeschooling means –

A. Postponing school until after the tennis years.
B. More time for your kid to practice tennis.
C. Freedom from math and science.
D. None of the above.

If you selected D, then you're on the right track if you decide to homeschool your tennis kid. The only tennis-related reason that should compel a parent to decide to homeschool is to achieve the scheduling flexibility the serious pursuit of tennis requires. Chris Decker coaches elite juniors at the Universal Tennis Academy in Marietta, Georgia. In 1996, when Decker came to Marietta, he didn't know a single player who was homeschooled for the sake of tennis. Now, there are 10 to 15 such players in Decker's academy alone.

Is Homeschooling Right for You?

Homeschooling is not a euphemism for dropping out. Neither should it mean reducing school hours and substituting more tennis. And don't try to rationalize. "Tennis teaches life skills, doesn't it? Besides, last summer after the tournament in Washington DC, Debbie and I visited the Smithsonian. Debbie learned a lot about history, didn't she?" Well, this doesn't cut it – and it's not homeschooling.

Good homeschooling means the parent has chosen to be a teacher, administrator, and parent all rolled into one. The parent has to maintain the same number of hours for academic teaching as a public or private school. For the kid, homeschooling means increased self-discipline and adjusting to a different schedule for socialization. When you and your child understand these basic tenets and can make the necessary adjustments, then, and only then, consider homeschooling.

The National Home Education Network (More info: nhen.org) is a good place to get a comprehensive understanding of what it takes to homeschool a child. There are hundreds of books to help navigate the world of homeschooling. Read a few so that you can make an informed choice. "The First Year of Homeschooling Your Child" by Linda Dobson; And "What about College?" by Cafi Cohen and Patrick Farenga; and the "Homeschooling Almanac" by Mary Leppert and Michael Leppert are some of the best-selling books on this subject.

Having decided to homeschool your kid, it's good to know you don't have to have mastery of every subject. There are all sorts of wonderful resources to help you – homeschool suppliers, web-sites, and academic tutors. There are also support organizations that will guide you in helping your kid develop socialization skills and tutors to teach subjects that may be hard for some parents. There are even helpers who will organize proms for homeschoolers!

Homeschooling is a legal education option in every state in the United States. While some colleges are more homeschool-friendly than others, homeschoolers routinely earn college scholarships and obtain admission to Ivy League schools like Harvard and Yale. Understanding state homeschooling laws, diligent record keeping, and taking the standardized tests are keys to homeschooling success.

Steps to Successful Homeschooling

It's not uncommon for kids to homeschool during the middle school years with the goal of jumpstarting their tennis. After a year or two of exclusive focus on tennis, they return to their regular public or private high school.

One can argue that the ideal years to begin homeschooling for tennis reasons are between grades 9 and 12. During younger years the intensity of the game is low and scheduling time for tennis is generally not a problem. It is during the high school years that a flexible schooling schedule will help the tennis kid train better. A high school freshman will also have sufficient tennis experience to decide whether she wants to pursue the development of her game seriously.

Before allowing a kid to pull out of public or private school, there is groundwork to be laid:

1. Know the state law: Become familiar with and ensure you are meeting all the requirements of your state's homeschooling laws (More info: unschooling.com). Georgia law requires that a parent possess minimum teaching credentials, maintain adequate homeschooling records, and teach a curriculum "equivalent" to that of the public schools. Call your state legislature to obtain current information.

2. NCAA and school requirements: The NCAA has specific core course guidelines for homeschooling. If your kid is aiming for a general or athletic college scholarship, ascertain the latest requirements from the NCAA (More info: ncaa.org). It may be a good idea to contact the admissions offices of select schools for information about their homeschooling policies.
3. Develop a support network: Homeschooling families in your area, Scouts, 4-H, YMCA, YWCA, and volunteer organizations are some ways your kid can receive the social benefits of homeschooling. Bring together homeschooling kids in your area who may be interested in tennis for group lessons. Join or form a local tennis team with kids from homeschools and public schools to encourage interaction.
4. Preparing to teach: Chart the required academic courses and identify subjects you are already qualified to teach. Learn about topics not familiar to you by taking courses at a community college or through computer-based or video-based training packages. Enlist the aid of tutors to teach subjects that are hard for you.
5. Standardized testing: The SAT (More info: collegeboard.com) and ACT (More info: act.org) tests not only help a homeschooler get into college, the test scores can be used to measure general educational development. During the freshman year, prepare a schedule of all the standardized tests your homeschooler will want to take over the next two to three years. Preparation and testing occurs during the sophomore and junior years, in time for college admissions.

Ultimately, homeschooling goes beyond education – it's a lifestyle choice. Sometimes homeschooled kids complain about feeling lonely. Other times a parent's circumstances may change making it impossible to dedicate the time necessary for homeschooling. Realize that it's okay to return to public school if things don't work out.

If homeschooling is working well for you, know that you're in illustrious company. Thomas Edison, famous photographer Ansel Adams, Frances Collins, leader of the Human Genome project, and Venus and Serena Williams are a few of the hundreds of famous homeschoolers.

College Tennis Scholarships

Top advice for tennis scholarship applicants? Keep your grades up! The kid doesn't have to be a star player to earn a tennis scholarship. Decent grades, a reasonable player record, and good sportsmanship may well land him a free ride through college, particularly if he keeps his options open – another state, a Division II college, partial scholarships, and so on.

Even if the kid has other plans and isn't remotely interested in college, encourage him to go through the college admission and scholarship processes. You never know – when the mailman delivers the actual offer to the door, the kid may just decide it's one he can't refuse.

True Cost of College

According to the College Board, the average cost of tuition and room and board at four-year public schools is $12,127 per year. Private schools run up to three times as much (More info: collegeboard.com).

Fortunately, Uncle Sam, community organizations, and private enterprises are all on your side when it comes to paying for college. Few students pay the "sticker price" and it's not uncommon for 60 to 75 percent of students to receive some sort of financial aid.

For starters, there are attractive federal tax breaks for saving for college. On average, $4,500 in financial aid is disbursed annually to every college student, totaling about $129 billion. Your tax dollars make up over $60 billion of this amount. It makes sense that you'd want to get some of it back as financial aid for your child.

The Numbers

There are over 310,000 kids playing high school tennis at nearly 9,800 high schools, according to a recent study by the National Federation of State High School Associations. Several tens-of-thousands of these are high school seniors looking forward to participating in college tennis.

Nearly 15,500 kids play tennis at 1,200 colleges. If we assume an annual graduation rate of 25 to 30 percent, this means over 4,200 freshman boys and girls are needed each year for college tennis teams.

The good news is that most college tennis players benefit from some form of financial aid. For example, NCAA Division-I schools alone have 1,260 scholarships for men and 2,480 for women. Say, we have 300 boys and 300 girls in the 18s becoming eligible for a national ranking. Estimating two-thirds are old enough for college, only 400 nationally ranked players are thus available for recruiting by Division-I coaches dangling 3,740 full scholarships.

Now you know why a decent ranking, even at the USTA section-level, will allow a player to pick and choose from the best colleges. The scales tip further in favor of this player when you include Division II and III programs.

The Road to College

Taking the necessary steps early will offer your child the greatest number of options and help him make sound decisions. The freshman year of high school is the time when parent, child, and coach should obtain information and begin to develop a roadmap. At the beginning of the senior year, your child will make his final decision. In the interim, the parent and coach can offer a lot of help to a kid on the road to college.

Getting into the college of choice is not a foregone conclusion. Stay on top of things and do the following:

1. *Collect information:* In the first year of high school, you and your child should absorb as much information as possible about the college admission and financial aid processes. Keep your options open and contact all major college associations – NCAA (More info: ncaa.org), NAIA (More info: naia.org), and NJCAA (More info: njcaa.org).
2. *Compile lists:* The NCAA and NAIA require certain core courses. Make a list of the nearly 15 or so core courses and be sure they are completed during high school. Consult a high school counselor and compile a list of at least 50 colleges from among the NCAA, NAIA, and NJCAA members that interest you. Contact the admissions office of these colleges to discuss any special needs – homeschool policies and so on.
3. *Preliminary tests:* Be sure the child takes the PSAT/NMSQT (More info: collegeboard.org) tests during the freshman and sophomore years. Use the reports to analyze your child's strengths and weaknesses and to prepare for the SAT. As a bonus, the PSAT results also automatically put your child in the running for the merit scholarships and corporate scholarships awarded by the National Merit Scholarship Corporation (NMSC. More info: nationalmerit.org).
4. *The All-important junior year:* The child should now take the SAT (More info: collegeboard.com) and ACT (More info: act.org) tests. Report scores to the NCAA Clearinghouse. Register with the NCAA Clearinghouse at the end of the junior year (More info: ncaa.org). Arrange recruiting visits to the colleges. Monitor core course selections.
5. *Apply:* During the child's senior year, finalize the college list and apply. The college coach may also help with the application. Find out

about private and local scholarships and apply for them. Include in your child's portfolio the following:

- The player's record. Generally coaches value results in USTA-sanctioned tournaments more than high school tennis results.
- A video of about six games in a match-play situation.
- Newspaper clippings and other media coverage.
- Letters of recommendation from both past and present coaches.
- Details of sponsorship by racket and apparel manufacturers and so on.

6. *Meet the coach:* Arrange recruiting visits to the colleges and get to know the coaches. Some tournaments, like the USTA Girls 18 Super National Hard Court Championship in San Jose, include a college coaches forum (More info: ustagirls.org). Tournament players are able to talk to coaches from dozens of colleges.

Show the coach your interest is genuine by contacting the school several times. Too many kids assume a coach just isn't interested in them, when, in reality the coach may be questioning the kid's interest because there's been insufficient follow-up.

7. *Final selection:* You may receive a National Letter of Intent from an NCAA-affiliated office or an offer letter directly from the school. Experts advise selecting a college based first on academic strength, then on the size and location of the school, the quality of the coach and team, graduation rate, and, finally, the scholarship money available. Don't let the best financial aid package unduly influence your decision. Scholarships are awarded on a year-by-year basis. Even if there is little or no money available for your child's freshman year, that doesn't mean there will be no money for subsequent years.

8. *After the high school graduation party*: Have the high school counselor mail final transcripts to the NCAA Clearinghouse and NAIA/ NJCAA colleges.

A lot of students have to work or take out student loans to pay for college, but with reasonable grades, a decent tennis-record, and an organized plan of action, your tennis kid can play his way through college.

13

Careers in Tennis

"Your dreams tell you what to do; your reason tells you how to do it."
JONAS SALK, developer of the polio vaccine.

A kid may excel at tennis. This does not automatically mean he has to take up tennis as a career. He may not even want to. A good tennis player can choose to become a scientist, entrepreneur, cop, or musician. Who's to say a top junior won't turn his tennis excellence into an ivy-league scholarship, major in business, and become a wildly successful entrepreneur? He might even surpass the fame and fortune of a World No. 1 tennis player.

That said, realize that tennis can play a major role in achieving success in any field. The self-discipline, focus, organizational skills, strategic thinking, physical fitness and, most importantly, friendships developed playing tennis are all invaluable, no matter what career path one ultimately follows.

Defining Career Success

Career counselors will tell you that kids who develop early career plans are most likely to succeed. Most kids start to weigh career options during their high school years. Grown-up support from the parent, coach, and career counselor can come in the form of helping the tennis kid develop a plan that includes at least four or five career options. Parents need to consider the financial implications of each choice – what will it take, financially, to prepare for and achieve each career option.

A chosen career path can affect just about everything: how much time you're willing to devote to a specific activity; what you read; what your hobbies and interests are; the people to whom you're attracted. Career planning experts advise their clients to think big and be prepared to adjust their plans as they move forward.

Any career plan should include a definition of success. That definition might include money and fame. Whatever you choose to include, don't forget to add a healthy dose of personal happiness and community service to your own definition of career success.

Teaching Professional

A player with even a modest playing record can aspire to be a great teaching professional. In fact, some of the most groundbreaking and respected coaches like Nick Bollettieri, Dennis Van der Meer, and Vic Braden had less than modest playing records.

To be successful, a tennis teacher must possess qualities more critical than a top playing record: keen observation and deduction skills; knowledge and love of the game; patience; the ability to motivate; and a capacity to focus on a single individual, even in a group setting. For teaching young children, one quality stands above all others – the ability to make lessons fun.

There are two ways to earn a tennis teaching credential – a certification from either the United States Professional Tennis Association (USPTA. More info: uspta.com) or the Professional Tennis Registry (PTR. More info: ptrtennis.org). A third reputable organization, Peter Burwash International (PBI. More info: pbitennis.com), offers education and also has a placement service that staffs tennis resorts worldwide.

Certification by USPTA

The USPTA certifies thousands of new teachers each year. Certification is earned on the basis of a two-day test offered more than 150 times a year in various cities.

There is a one-day workshop and stroke analysis before the actual testing begins. Written portions of the test can be taken that same evening and the on-court test the next day. Testing includes teaching a group lesson, a private lesson, and analysis of grips and strokes. The application fee for testing is $175 and the prorated annual dues are about $240. Certification is available in three levels based upon the number of years of teaching experience – Pro 3, 2 and 1 – with level 1 certification requiring the most years of experience.

Junior tennis players, high school coaches, and others who want to teach part-time may find the USPTA‘s certification for Developmental Coaches a lower cost alternative. This certification is earned by attending a one-day training session and annual dues are $125.

Certification by PTR

The PTR offers an education designed by remarkable coach and founder, Dennis Van der Meer. The application and annual dues are about half of that of the USPTA. Members are certified as Associate Instructor, Instructor, or Professional on the basis of performance in the organization's testing. Many pros earn both USPTA and PTR certifications.

The PTR has a special membership category for juniors ages 14 to 17 who aspire to become tennis teachers. As Junior Affiliate Members, young players serve as apprentices to certified professionals and attend PTR workshops.

Training by PBI

PBI, founded and run by Peter Burwash, an accomplished player and respected coach, is a tennis management firm that trains tennis teachers and places them at tennis resorts worldwide. An NTRP 5.0 rating is generally expected of the recruits.

The month-long training includes classes in club and resort management, in addition to teaching tennis techniques. Pre-employment training is free except for room and board expenses. After completion of training, candidates are employed by PBI as hotel pros to run its tennis programs at resorts.

Professional Tennis Management

Skilled tennis players can combine their interest in tennis with a degree in Professional Tennis Management (PTM), a gateway to career opportunities in the tennis industry. PTM graduates also earn certification as teaching professionals.

Learning about the business side of tennis makes a PTM graduate better prepared to assume the duties of teaching professional, tennis director, club manager, camp director, pro-shop manager, tennis industry executive, or community recreation manager. A PTM degree is also useful if you want to start your own business, such as owning or leasing a tennis club, becoming a supplier of tennis goods or a builder of courts.

Three schools currently offer graduate-level PTM programs accredited by the USPTA: Ferris State University (More info: ferris.edu), Methodist College (More info: methodist.edu), and Tyler Junior College (More info: tjc.edu). The Queens University of Charlotte (More info: queens.edu) offers a PTM program accredited by the PTR, and available to college-age students as well as adults.

Tennis organizations like the USTA (More info: usta.com), the ATP (More info: atptennis.com), and the WTA (More info:

wtatour.com) also offer attractive opportunities. Networking is crucial for both learning about career opportunities and landing a job. Volunteering and internships with these organizations can result in valuable contacts.

School Sports Management

College and high school athletics represent a huge segment of the sports industry. Almost every academic institution has an athletic program. The NCAA (More info: ncaa.org), NAIA (More info: naia.org), and NJCAA (More info: njcaa.org) together have nearly 2,000 member colleges and nearly half of them offer tennis programs.

Of the nearly 17,500 high schools (More info: nfhs.org) in the United States, over 55 percent run tennis programs. Most jobs in high school sports management are far from glamorous, but high school sports attract more fans than do their collegiate and professional counterparts. High schools spend about six times as much on sports programs as does the NCAA.

Many sports industry executives began their careers in school athletics. Coaching a tennis team is just one of the many exciting opportunities available. Most athletic departments have a variety of staff positions, including athletic director, facilities manager, tickets director, marketing director, fund raising manager, student-athlete affairs, and many more.

Most jobs in this field require a degree in liberal arts, education, kinesiology, sports administration, or business management. Again, volunteering or interning with an athletic department can open the door to these positions.

Sports Marketing

Love of sports is just one of the qualifications needed to succeed in sports marketing. A bachelor's degree in law, business management or advertising, combined with solid experience, is key to doing well in a sports marketing career.

Some of the larger sports marketing companies that have an active involvement in tennis include IMG (More info: imgworld.com), William Morris Agency (More info: wma.com), and SFX Sports Group (More info: clearchannel.com). Sports marketing firms usually focus on some or all of three functions: athlete representation, corporate marketing, and event marketing. Companies like IMG have a fourth component – managing sports events.

Athlete Representation

Aside from hard-nosed contract negotiations on behalf of a professional athlete, representation for financial counsel, endorsement marketing, and public relations are becoming more prevalent. A representative may do all of these things for a client or choose to specialize in one aspect.

Between state requirements and fierce competition, breaking in as an independent player agent can be daunting. Fortunately, there are hundreds of medium-to-large sports marketing companies hungry for quality recruits.

Corporate Marketing

An agency's work consists of developing and executing a marketing program that utilizes sports and sports personalities to market a company or product. A sports marketing program can include a variety of components, from simple projects such as designing and manufacturing sports giveaways or distributing match schedules, to much grander undertakings like developing a sports-related advertising campaign, naming a stadium, or garnering a celebrity endorsement for the company's products.

Working for a college athletic department or local sports team will provide invaluable experience for almost any sports marketing career. Find out what you're good at, and what you enjoy most, by exploring various departments, from operations to creative design to management. Understand the game, not just the statistics. Know the players and the sports media; stay on the cutting edge; be informed about current industry trends and where they might lead in the future.

Event Management and Marketing

Managing and marketing major tournaments like the Tennis Masters Series require considerable experience and expertise. Millions of dollars are spent on these events and a large team is required to manage them. A typical event team includes the Event Director, Marketing Director, Sales Director, Director of Operations, and Client Services Coordinator.

The Event Director oversees the entire event, works to secure major sponsorship from corporations, and signs up star players. The Sales Manager sells advertising space and coordinates promotional campaigns and ticket sales. The Client Services Coordinator is responsible for responding to the needs of sponsors, advertising clients, and players and also oversees corporate ticket sales. The Marketing Director coordinates advertising and promotion in advance of the event.

Along with event staff, many hundreds of volunteers are needed to make any such tournament a success. Volunteering is a great way to build a resume and will give you an up-close-and-personal view of event management and marketing. It can also lead to a wealth of industry contacts.

Tennis Officiating

If you've always wanted to get back at those arrogant professional players, there's a career track that's perfect for you – tennis officiating. Just kidding. And so is the USTA when it calls its officials "Friends at court." Just ask a certain fellow named McEnroe.

Tennis officiating is certainly not a full-time job, and there's no telling when the officials' duties will be taken over by a robot. While it lasts, though, and some jobs certainly will, officiating is a great way for tennis enthusiasts to stay connected to the game while basking in the authority on-court.

A tournament requires a variety of officials: Line Umpires to call assigned lines; Net Umpires to call the nets, of course; a Chair Umpire to call the score and oversee the Line and the Net Umpires. A Roving Umpire is a kind of mobile Chair Umpire who monitors multiple courts. And then there is the tournament's ultimate official – the Referee.

To get started, you must first pass a written test given by the USTA Officials Department (More info: usta.com) to qualify as a Provisional Umpire. An upwardly mobile official then becomes a Sectional Umpire by attending school, testing, and umpiring a set number of matches.

After the Sectionals, the process is the same for each higher stage – Intercollegiate Umpire, USTA Umpire, National Umpire and, at the top, a Professional Umpire. All of the officials you see working at ATP and WTA tournaments have spent many years developing their skills at amateur tournaments.

During the rookie years, pay is the pits. Days are always long, hot, and hard. However, the deep sense of elation that comes from umpiring a tough match can be fully understood and felt only by members of this exclusive club. As any umpire will tell you, it's an extraordinary feeling!

Athletic Trainer

The trainer's goal is to keep the player in top physical condition and prevent injuries. If a player does sustain an injury, it's the trainer's job to design treatment programs and oversee rehab. The position is variously called a Physical Conditioning Trainer, Strength and Conditioning Trainer, and Personal Fitness Trainer.

The American Medical Association recognizes trainers as allied health professionals. The National Athletic Trainer's Association (NATA. More info: nata.org) primarily certifies trainers. The minimum educational requirement is a bachelor's degree, with the completion of a program in athletic training. NATA also requires passing a multi-part examination and hundreds of hours of supervised experience, usually working with head trainers at their colleges. Many states require trainers to be registered or licensed.

Most jobs are in college and high school sports. Health clubs, large corporations, and tennis organizations like the ATP and WTA also hire athletic trainers. Once again, a great way to get started is by volunteering or working part-time while in school.

The best-paying jobs are held by those who work with professional players. As you might expect, these positions are also the toughest to find. Trainers who work with tennis players find it useful to obtain membership in an allied organization called the National Strength and Conditioning Association (More info: nsca-lift.org).

Sports Entrepreneur

Charles Hoeveler came to the Stanford Business School on an NCAA postgraduate scholarship, the result of academic and athletic achievement at Dartmouth College, where he was Eastern Intercollegiate tennis champion. A 1969 grad, Hoeveler has not only kept his competitive spirit alive by winning national Father-Son titles with Charles Jr., Hoeveler Sr. has also turned his passion for tennis into a thriving enterprise.

Back in the 70s and 80s, sports camps were mom-and-pop shows. Organizers relied on flyers and faxes to get the word out about an upcoming camp. Enrollment was basically local.

Charles Hoeveler changed all that, bringing together multi-sport and multi-city camps under the umbrella of a single company – US Sports & Specialty Camps. Instead of flyers and faxes, Hoeveler relies on a top-notch web site for registration and camp administration, along with professionally designed brochures. A sponsorship arrangement allows him to use the world-class Nike brand name for his camps.

Today, US Sports & Specialty Camps pulls in nearly $17 million in annual revenue, offering 26 different sports and specialty programs serving tens of thousands of campers each year. Charles Hoeveler's entrepreneurial spirit has enabled him to create the world's largest sports camp operation.

Tennis is legion with stories of entrepreneurs who transformed their love of the game into successful products and businesses. Rene Lacoste, the French champion, created an equipment and apparel empire based on two inventions – the metal racket and the trademark "crocodile" tennis polo shirt. Howard Head invented the metal ski and later the oversized tennis racket, revolutionizing both sports.

Now if only someone would come up with a robot that could pick up tennis balls and return them to the basket. Any young tennis-entrepreneurs-in-waiting out there?

Tournament Owner

Are you a good enough salesperson to convince your town that it needs a tennis tournament? Do you know any corporate movers and shakers who will sponsor your event? If you answered yes to these questions, you're on your way to becoming a true tennis impresario.

Hands-on experience while developing expertise in various tournament functions is critical. A bachelor's degree in law or business will make the job easier. You can hire an experienced sports marketing company to worry about the marketing and operation of the event. In this business, organization and thorough planning will make the inevitable last-minute emergencies easier to cope with – a star player falling sick, for instance.

Owning a tournament will not make you rich, but if you're willing to take risks, owning a tournament can be a fulfilling experience, year after year. To get started, contact the appropriate tennis organization – the USTA (More info: usta.com) for amateur tournaments, the ATP (More info: atptennis.com) for men's professionals, and the WTA (More info: wtatour.com) for the women's professionals.

For example, to own a new WTA tournament, the prospective owner must apply to the WTA and submit a $5,000 fee. Half the fee is refundable if the WTA rejects the application. The WTA approves applications based on, among other things, geographical location, a site check, security considerations, the applicant's financial solvency.

The prospective owner is required to show proof that he has the funds necessary to operate the tournament and pay the total prize money.

Owning a tournament beats dueling it out on court anytime.

Professional Player

Turning professional can be a momentous step in a young player's career, but the actual process of "turning pro" is really fairly basic. For instance, the entry form for the USTA Professional Circuit has two check-boxes – "Pro" and "Amateur." Check the "Pro" box and voila! You're a pro!

A handful of new professionals earn top rankings and big prize monies quickly. Others may simply have to dig in for a few years on the tour – traveling and competing, gaining enough experience to be able to hit the spotlight. In either case, before turning pro, learn how the professional tours operate and understand the adjustments that need to be made when transitioning from amateur to professional status. This will help make the professional experience rewarding and enjoyable.

Prize Money vs. Lunch Money

Becoming a professional player means you have chosen to make your living playing tennis. This is a lot different from playing tennis for recreation. Many new pros quickly discover that "prize" money is really lunch money.

In junior competition expenses are low and there's no problem getting sponsors; in college a player has financial aid and scholarships, but a new professional is on his own. Aside from free apparel and rackets, the player pays for his flights, hotels, laundry, and meals.

Tour insiders say most pro players spend over $30,000 annually in airfare alone. Add the cost of a traveling coach, hotel, food, and stringing jobs and a professional player is looking at $50,000 just to break even.

A professional tournament with $25,000 total prize money will net the winner about $3,600. If the rookie can't get past the first round, he earns a few hundred dollars and will be seriously in the red when you include flight and hotel expenses. It's easy to see why young professionals may need financial support to sustain themselves during the initial years, as they get their feet wet and gain valuable professional experience.

Unless one rises to a top ranking quickly or has earned a sponsorship deal up-front, most professionals have to develop a sound financial plan for the early years. Having a good financial plan will help junior better focus on tennis. With financial support in place, matches will becomes less about the paycheck and more about the game. Ultimately, this will improve rankings and earnings.

When To Turn Pro

Lleyton Hewitt played competitive football along with tennis until he reached the 12s. After playing in a few high-level international tennis tournaments and doing well, he decided to focus exclusively on tennis. Soon thereafter, at age 17, Hewitt turned pro.

The decision to turn professional should be made based on clinical assessment rather than at the gut level. Many top juniors watch professionals playing on TV and decide they want to follow in their footsteps. Loving to cook at home is no guarantee of success in the restaurant business. New professionals are often surprised by the wide chasm between the nature of junior competition and the professional tour.

Instead, assuming the player is building a credible record at the regional and national level from the 14s onwards, huddle the decision-making team every now and then. The kid, parent, coach, athletic trainer, and other mentors should meet to make a clinical assessment of the following:

✓ *Ability:* As noted, success at the professional level is more dependent on ability than on effort. It takes tremendous work to maintain a top 100 professional ranking, but what differentiates No. 1 from No. 100 is more competence than effort. Judge your kid's ability based on consistent performance in high-level competition. Make allowance for potential improvements based on physical growth, high performance coaching, and tour experience. If the team is convinced the kid is ready for professional competition at all levels – strokes, strategy, physical conditioning, and mental maturity – he is one step closer to turning pro.

✓ *Financial Plan:* Are agents and corporate sponsors showing interest in the kid? Can a sponsorship deal be lined up at this time? If not, is there a plan to cover expenses for a year or two?

If the decision is not to turn pro at this time, go back to the drawing board. Focus on skill and win-loss improvement and on attracting the attention of agents and sponsors. Make another assessment in six months.

On the other hand, if the team believes the player is ready, go for it. Watch out, Hewitt, there's a new kid on the block!

Amateur Status

Believe it or not, there's at least one major perk to being an amateur – college athletic scholarships. If a player plans to attend college or is currently attending college, accepting prize money may automatically rule him ineligible for NCAA athletic scholarships (More info: ncaa.org). This may not be a big deal if a player is doing well as a professional and intends to stick with the pro tour.

Some new professionals, though, give the tour a try for a couple of years and, if the going isn't so good, they may decide to return to college. In that case, be prepared for the fall-out from loss of amateur status.

In fact, there's a better way to try out on the professional circuit without risking loss of amateur status. Play the USTA professional circuit as an amateur (More info: usta.com). Players are offered the opportunity to declare amateur or professional status at each event.

As an amateur, you cannot accept prize money. The consolation is that you earn valuable professional ranking points that can show how well you're doing on the pro circuit. Whether an amateur wins or not, he's eligible to receive reimbursable expenses, in keeping with NCAA guidelines (More info: ncaa.org).

Ranking vs. Earning

The good news is that no one can stop you from winning a tournament. The prize money you win is the same, whether you're currently ranked No. 100 or No. 1. However, private deals – endorsements, corporate sponsorships, tournament appearance fees and such work a little differently.

Private deals are based on a subjective combination of ranking and the perception of a player's marketability. No business-savvy executive can afford to ignore a player's ranking when evaluating a private deal. All showmanship and no game won't consistently entice the paying public. One has to understand that for the corporate dealmaker, this is essentially an investment and his goal is to maximize the return on that investment.

For an advertising campaign, a player ranked No. 15 may be perceived to have the ability to move products off the shelf better than another player who is ranked No. 10. Guess what? It's likely, Mr. 15 will get a better endorsement deal. Similarly, a tournament director may believe that a certain Ms. A's appearance at the tournament is key to drawing the public. In the tournament director's eyes, Ms. A would justifiably command a larger appearance fee.

These examples may seem a bit too cut and dried and dealmakers will tell you things are never quite so simple. All the same, if junior is aware of the business side of the professional game, he will make a better adjustment to life on the circuit.

Getting Started in Professional Tennis

The USTA Professional Circuit (More info: usta.com) is the ideal place to start for new professionals and amateurs who want to test their readiness for the professional tour. The USTA holds about 100 professional tournaments each year.

The prize money is a good indicator of the level of competition you can expect. At the lower end, the $10,000 total prize money events feel like a frat house, with college and junior players competing to earn valuable professional ranking points. Guess how much of that prize money goes to the winner – about $1,000. The good news is if you're an amateur and can't accept the winnings, at least you won't lose sleep over it.

A player starts with zero points. Take heart, you can only go up from there. A player with no points is accepted into a preliminary competition called the qualifying draw. An event that has 32 positions in the main draw may have another 128 positions in the qualifying draw. Acceptance into qualifying is determined by a player's rank. If more people have signed up than there are spots available, acceptance into qualifying is determined by a player's record in junior competition – National rank, ITA Division 1, National 18s, National 16s, Sectional Opens and so on, in that order.

Basically, rookies duke it out in the qualifiers and the top four or so earn entry into the main draw of 32. If a player has earned sufficient points from previous tournaments, he earns direct acceptance into the main draw of 32.

As you accumulate more ranking points you begin to gain entry to the next higher level of competition. At the highest level of the USTA Professional Circuit are the $50,000 to $75,000 events.

ATP and WTA

This is the real deal for an aspiring professional player – the ATP (More info: atptennis.com) for the young man, and WTA (More info: wtatour.com) for the young woman.

Like the USTA Professional Circuit, the ATP and WTA operate tournaments in various categories based on prize money. The WTA tour has 60-plus tier events, four Grand Slam events, and a tour championship. The total prize money starts at $110,000 for a Tier 5 event and rises to $3 million for the year-ending tour championship.

The ATP tour makes 70-odd tournament stops, including the four Grand Slam events, nine Masters Series, and the end-of-year Tennis Masters Cup. The total prize money starts at $380,000 for an International Series event and scales to upwards of $3.70 million for the year-ending Tennis Masters Cup.

The four Grand Slams are at the top of the tennis food chain, offering winners the biggest prize-money catch. Based upon points earned in USTA Professional Circuit events and later in ATP or WTA events, a player either gains direct entry to the tournaments' main draw or may have to start in the qualifying draw.

Life on the Tour

The travel opportunities, earnings, friendships, and media attention are all worth soaking up, but turn pro on the basis of clinical assessment rather than emotion. Have a sound financial plan to support the initial learning curve. These things are key to making the player's professional years some of the best years of his life.

Sports Media

Once limited to the sports page of the local newspaper and a few radio and television reports, sports media now includes glossy magazines, entire television networks, and the Internet. Sports Illustrated, Tennis magazine, CNNSI.com, ESPN, IMG, and the ubiquitous sports talk radio shows are all examples of how wide the reach of sports media has become.

A print and online media team is typically comprised of sports editors, writers, photographers, advertising salespeople, and graphic artists. For radio and television shows, there's the show host, the producer, and the engineering and camera support staff.

Most specialized jobs require a degree in journalism. Popular players often find their way into broadcasting because of their celebrity and knowledge of the game. In 1980, tennis player Mary Carillo was near the end of a professional career. She was watching a tournament at Madison Square Garden when a broadcaster asked her to comment on the match.

"I had played early in the evening, and they needed somebody to fill some time," says Carillo. "I was lively, opinionated and cracking wise." A television producer saw the broadcast and hired Carillo for the USA Network. She now points to a willingness to learn about the media business and thorough preparation before a match as important keys to her success.

14

Building a Tennis Community

"Take your passion and make it happen."
FLASHDANCE, lyrics from the song What a Feeling.

Let's start with a worst-case scenario. Your community, umm... Pleasantville...has no courts and no players. Worst of all nobody is interested in tennis, except you. What do you do? How do you pique community interest? And how can you go about building a tennis-loving community?

Hello, USTA. The United States Tennis Association is the governing body of tennis in the United States (More info: usta.com). The USTA consists of 17 geographical sections. Sections have districts and community tennis associations (CTAs). Many thousands of volunteers and professionals run these organizations, coming together to support tennis programs all over the country.

The USA Tennis Pathway is the largest initiative ever launched to promote and develop the growth of tennis in the United States. The USTA spearheads this task force with a broad coalition of industry-wide organizations, including tennis equipment manufacturers, training associations, parks and recreation departments, pro-tour associations, collegiate tennis, and allied organizations.

Tennis is the only sport played by 3 to 70-plus-year- olds. The Pathway supports a healthy community by encouraging active living for all ages.

Linking with the USTA

If you're a coach or a tennis player, chances are you're already linked to the United States Tennis Association (USTA). For a parent new to tennis, linking with the USTA can help locate organizations in your area dedicated to promoting tennis and find programs to develop a tennis pathway for your junior.

If your area is not served by a CTA, the USTA can help you start one by providing financial grants and volunteer support. You don't have to be a tennis player to develop a CTA. A start-up group helps, but one passionate individual is enough to get started on the road to building a tennis-loving community (More info: usta.com).

Working with Parks & Recreation

Many communities run tennis programs on public courts, but the courts may not be easily accessible or may need repairs. Current tennis programs may not be targeting all sections of the community. If yours is such a community, or even otherwise, it helps if the CTA understands the various public agencies involved.

Public courts are generally built and maintained by parks and recreation departments, with youth sports programs run by the local community center. Parks and recreation, community center, and CTA are the agencies involved in tennis in your area. A good working relationship between this triad of organizations is essential.

Do your homework. Find out what, if any, tennis programs are now offered. How are they funded? Generally, local tax dollars pay the community center staff and participant fees fund the sports program. Determine what tennis-specific gaps exist in current programs. Are there programs to support a junior's growth from beginning level through high school? Perhaps an after-school tennis program is what your community needs.

Understand how the CTA can work with parks and recreation and the community center to meet these needs by contributing tennis-specific organizational expertise, volunteers, and access to awards and grants.

Developing Tennis Facilities

It's not rocket science. Spearhead a drive to build courts in your neighborhood. Offer a free clinic. Within a few weeks you'll find Jennifer, Johnnie, and friends duking it out after school with rackets and a ball. Access to a tennis court is a top reason kids get hooked on tennis.

A study of tennis courts by the USTA and ASBA recommends courts be available within six miles, or within a 15 to 20 minute drive, for most players in the area (More info: Tennis Courts by Carol Shaner). The study estimates the number of public and private courts needed for various populations (Table 14.1).

In planning indoor courts, a good rule of thumb is that most markets can support one indoor court for every 10,000 people. Check the court inventory in your community. If the number comes up short, it's time to rumble.

Bring together all the groups and organizations with a vested interest in developing tennis facilities in the area and create a CTA

Table 14.1

Population	Number of Courts
15,000	20
25,000	30
50,000	50
100,000	80
250,000	130
500,000	210
750,000	270
1,000,000	320
1,250,000	360
1,500,000	400
More than 1,500,000	1 per 4000

Special Interest Group. Here are a few possibilities:

✓ Real estate agents. For many people, local availability of courts is a serious factor in deciding where to live. In the United States, this number is large and the people are affluent enough to get the real estate guys excited about your project. A global survey of tournament attendees conducted by the ATP is revealing. Nearly 47 percent of spectators have earnings that exceed $100,000 annually, and a whopping 66 percent are college graduates. It's safe to assume that numbers in the United States are even higher.

✓ Court builders in your area. Contact a court builders association for references. The US Tennis Court & Track Builders Association (More info: ustctba.org) is one such organization.

✓ Parks and recreation department.

✓ Tennis club management from other neighborhoods.

✓ Professional tennis teachers.

Facility formats include public courts, private courts, and tennis clubs. The current popularity of tennis in your community, potential for growth, the average age and income of the population will determine which of these formats will ultimately stick.

Maybe a club entrepreneur believes you have a viable community in which to build a tennis club. Perhaps the parks and recreation department is able to develop a good site for courts in a city park or to add more courts at an existing site.

There is also a middle-of-the-road option between the swanky private club and a tax-paid, free-for-all public court. The City of Monterey, in California, has developed a highly successful public court system that is paid for by access and clinic fees. The Monterey Tennis Center opens its six courts to the public for an annual access fee of $200. Included are all the perks you'd expect from a private tennis club: ball machines, a certified coach, and a pro shop.

Building a Tennis Court

Many tennis stars like Andre Agassi, Lleyton Hewitt, and Andy Roddick had tennis courts in their backyards while growing up. You probably know the fabled story of Agassi's boyhood court.

Andre's dad was so single-minded about his ultimate goal to raise Andre to be a champion, he didn't even see the interior of their first Las Vegas home. While Mom was checking out the carpets and appliances, Dad Mike was outside measuring the backyard to ensure it was big enough for a tennis court. He built the court himself, using the construction experience he acquired working at a Chicago building site.

If you're lucky enough to have a large backyard that can support a tennis court and want one built, great. If not, don't lose heart. Look for a site in your community sub-division or a nearby park. Remember the organizational triad: parks and recreation, local community center and CTA. Add a motivated court builder to the mix and you could soon have a conveniently located court at your sub-division or park.

Today there are a good number of builders whose bread-and-butter is building tennis courts. The American Sports Builders Association (ASBA. More info: sportsbuilders.org) mentioned earlier is a good starting point. The association can refer contractors in your area who can undertake a detailed feasibility study for you.

The project may be feasible space-wise, but for a backyard court consider the sound and light impact inside your house and on your neighbors. The insistent, throbbing pop of a ball-machine can quickly drive neighbors to the courts – the kind with prosecutors and judges.

For doubles tennis, the court size is 36 by 78 feet. Adding the playing area, clearances, and room for construction, the ASBA suggests a minimum site size of 70 by 120 feet. Hard courts can be had for anywhere from $18,000 to $40,000, depending upon the specific construction. An optional cushioning layer topping the hard court adds $5,000 to $25,000 to the cost.

Because of the fine slopes needed for drainage on the court surface, building a backyard court is probably not a do-it-yourself project. However, you can see substantial savings if you choose to work alongside the contractor. In the design phase, be sure to plan for plenty of power outlets for ball-machines.

Developing Volunteers

Volunteers are the backbone of any tennis-loving community. Community service doesn't have to mean giving up leisure time. Volunteering can fit easily between career and family and can enhance – rather than replace – a family's interests and the time they spend together.

A family can have a great time at a local tennis event on a Saturday afternoon. Dad can help out at the refreshment stand while Mom staffs the information desk. Jennifer is competing hard in the 10s, and the 6-year-old is having a grand time being a ball runner.

Recruiting Volunteers

Recruiting and keeping volunteers motivated is job one for a community tennis association. Volunteers give their time because they enjoy what they're doing. Offer them jobs they really want to do and remember what motivates them to volunteer.

You'll find that volunteers are motivated by all sorts of factors, including a desire to feel needed, share a skill, get to know a community, learn something new, gain recognition, become an "insider," explore a career, gain status, or simply fill up free time. Volunteers will continue to serve as long as they are given recognition and feel that their efforts are making a difference.

The USTA (More info: USTA Guide for Community Tennis Associations) suggests the following as places to find effective volunteers:

- Schools. Contact the principal or the Parent Teacher Association.
- Colleges. Contact the dean of students.
- Churches and Temples. Contact the pastor, rabbi, or priest.
- Professional Associations. Lawyers, tax advisors, and bookkeepers are always needed. Contact the president of the bar association and CPA group.

- Veterans organizations. VFW, AMVETS, and America Legion. Contact the post commander.
- Social and Business Organizations. Rotary and Lions. Contact the executive in charge.
- Special Interest Groups. Contact camera, sports, literary, music, or other types of hobby and special interest clubs.

Training Volunteers

Now that you've successfully recruited volunteers, keep them happy and effective by providing education and growth opportunities. For example, even a non-playing parent can be trained to serve as a court monitor, roving the tournament courts assuring the rules of the game are followed. Contact your local section and district office of the USTA for help with training (More info: usta.com).

Developing Tennis Teachers in Your Community

When your community lacks trained tennis teachers, your best bet may be to hold a low-cost Developmental Coaches workshop. The USTA works in conjunction with the USPTA and PTR to bring the one-day workshops to your community.

The workshop will train recreational and high school players who want to teach part time. The goal is to develop tennis teachers who can coach the USA 1-2-3 and USA Team Tennis programs.

Finding Money for Community Tennis

A new CTA is no different from a start-up company making the venture capital rounds. Discovering and developing funding sources; making plan presentations and demonstrating value; asking for the check; and keeping investors frequently apprised of progress are all integral to any business enterprise. Perform them with passion and a smile. Think of money sources as customers.

Fortunately, a CTA doesn't need a whole lot of money to get off the ground and can be started by one interested individual. You will, however, want to recruit people with fund raising experience for your board of directors as soon as possible. As your programs grow, fund raising expertise will be essential.

Preliminary Steps

Before making the money rounds, incorporate the CTA as a tax-exempt, not-for-profit corporation. In many states incorporation involves submitting a form to the secretary of state's office. Separate forms for tax-exempt status are also required by the IRS and state tax boards.

Total filing fees for incorporation and tax-exempt status should run about $30 to $40. If a local tax law professional is willing to donate time, he can help you with incorporation and in forming the initial board of directors. You can also refer to the many excellent self-help books published by Nolo Press (More info: nolo.com) at your local library.

If you want your CTA to be affiliated with the USTA, submit the Organizational Membership and Registration forms. The USTA offers grant money, expertise, and volunteer support for starting and running a CTA, so it's probably a good idea to become a USTA affiliate. Contact your USTA section office to get all the information you'll need (More info: usta.com). There is a $25 membership fee for organizations, but the out-of-pocket expenses you incur can be reimbursed once the CTA receives its initial grant.

Getting a few members signed up early will help demonstrate community interest in the CTA. Post flyers on community, court, and online bulletin boards.

Money Sources

There are many sources of funding for community programs, but there are always more needy agencies asking for help than there are grant dollars available. You can make the fund-raising process less intimidating with a few key strategies:

Start with the sources you know.

As a tennis organization, you're most likely to find support from players, clubs, and tennis shops in your area, as well as the USTA sectional office. Initiate starter league play for the players and charge a user fee. Have local clubs and tennis shops sponsor your web site. Tap into the USTA's grants and awards program.

Extend this initial network and get some organizational members involved. For example, John, who is a league player, is an executive at a local corporation. The company has a community outreach program. Ask John to speak on your behalf and help you sell your CTA to the folks who head that outreach program.

Enlist support of non-tennis foundations

Over 70,000 foundations nationwide grant money to non-profit organizations (More info: fdncenter.org). Investigate ways you can incorporate local non-tennis issues into your programs to greatly increase the grant options available to you.

Tenacity, Inc is a great example. This organization successfully tackles issues related to after-school hours and low academic performance and combines them with tennis opportunities. Tenacity operates an excellent after-school tennis and academics program that serves disadvantaged youth from neighborhoods in the Boston Area (More info: tenacity.org).

Enlist the support of the Women's Sports Foundation's Community Action Program by adding programs targeting girls' participation (More info: womenssportsfoundation.org).

Take advantage of in-kind support

Donation of products and services are just as beneficial as cash. Goods and services you don't have to buy or rent can save you a bundle. Here are a few:

- Tennis courts from parks and recreation, schools and colleges. Even private clubs may be able to donate court-time for an occasional tournament or fund-raising event.
- Rackets, balls, mobile net, and other equipment and supplies. Talk to your USTA section or a manufacturer's regional representative.
- Help with promotional materials and publicity.
- Professional services: legal, tax, and computers.
- Meeting rooms.
- Instruction by local pros.
- Local restaurants, pizza parlors, ice-cream shops, and water-bottlers.

Hold a fund-raising event

A special event can do wonders to supplement your budget. Tennis socials, an afternoon car wash, or a formal dinner can all work. Keep in mind your community's culture and interests.

The key to a successful fundraiser is to reduce out-of-pocket expenses by generating in-kind support for the event. As your CTA matures you'll find volunteers who specialize in and enjoy raising funds and planning events.

Grants, Awards and Incentives from the USTA

The USTA's main source of income is the US Open. A portion of earnings is funneled back to the community associations as program grants, awards, and incentive money.

A new CTA that achieves set goals and diligently maintains records can generate up to 15 percent of its annual budget in monies from the USTA. A mature CTA will need to generate additional money from other sources. Memberships, program user fees, fundraisers, and grants from other foundations are all potential resources.

USTA grants are offered for a period of one year and generally range from $200 to $1,500. This may not seem like a lot of money, but for a start-up CTA, it also offers the credibility of a national organization. This is critical when talking to other sponsors and foundations.

Grants

✓ CTA Start-up and Expansion: For creating and expanding a CTA, including incorporation fees, administrative expenses, rental of facilities, cost of equipment, membership expansion and so on.

✓ Programming Start-up and Expansion: For introducing and growing the USA Tennis Pathway programs including USA Tennis 1-2-3, Adult leagues, Junior leagues with an educational component, school tennis, and wheelchair and special population programs.

✓ Court Refurbishing: The Adopt-a-Court program funds up to $2,500 from the USTA National office, representing 5 to 20 percent of the total cost of repairing and upgrading a public or school court. The program requires a matching contribution at the USTA sectional level.

Awards

✓ The USA Tennis & Education Foundation helps fund USA Tennis National Junior Tennis Leagues (NJTL) and programs with an educational component in addition to tennis.

Incentives

USA Team Tennis is a league program with adult and junior components. Team coaches are eligible for a $4.00 incentive for each league player. The area coordinator, who oversees all teams in the area, is eligible for a stipend. Based on the number of teams in a given location, this stipend can be as much as $1,000.

Keep in mind that these programs can change from time to time. Your area section coordinator is your best bet for up-to-date information (More info: usta.com).

Grants from other foundations

Most sponsors like to know they're part of a larger group. It also makes good sense not to rely on a single foundation for support. Canvas support from as many organizations as you can, both local and national (More info: fdncenter.org). The Maureen Connolly Brinker Tennis Foundation (More info: mcbtennis.org) and the United States Professional Tennis Association (More info: uspta.com) are just two examples of national groups that support tennis at the local level.

Tennis Programs for the Community

Type of league: Adult or junior? Format: Round robin or elimination rounds? Which is better: Team or Individuals? What if you're the only one who's ever held a tennis racket in your town, population 3,040? How can you sustain a CTA when you can't get a single person to face you at the net? Relax. I mean it. USA Tennis Pathway to the rescue!

"Tennis for Everyone" is their motto. The smart folks at Pathway have not only designed a blueprint to make it happen in your community, they've also come up with four key words to help you remember the plan: TRY, LEARN, PLAY, and COMPETE (More info: usta.com). Okay, now repeat after me.

TRY: USA Tennis Free for All

Getting your community interested in tennis will be a big part of your association's success. USA Tennis Free for Alls are generally one-day events to introduce new players to the sport or get former players back in the swing of things. Include a free lessons blitz, games, drills, and social play.

LEARN: USA Tennis 1-2-3

This is a low-cost introductory instructional program for players of all ages. The program consists of six sessions, totaling at least nine hours, designed to teach the basics of the game in a fun, active, and encouraging group environment. Participants also get to meet new friends and potential playing partners.

PLAY: USA Team Tennis

Kids love to be with other kids. That's the idea behind USA Team Tennis (Youth). It takes an individual sport and turns it into a team activity set in a relaxed round robin format. The program offers kids an opportunity to test their newly acquired skills in leagues that emphasize fun, fitness, and friends. Kids get involved in a healthy, active sport and learn the importance of teamwork.

The adult component of this format, USA Team Tennis (Adult), is guaranteed to provide hours of match-play experience to a new player in a laid-back setting.

COMPETE: USA Tournament/ Scholastic Tennis

Now you're getting serious in terms of tennis competition.

Scholastic Tennis

Each year over 310,000 boys and girls play on varsity teams representing their high schools. They may also qualify for league, county, and state championships operated by the state athletic association. To start a league in your local high school, contact the USTA section office to find out ways to encourage the local school board to act.

Tournament Tennis

Welcome to the world of the US Open and its lesser-known siblings. Thousands of tournaments take place each year. Many are sanctioned by tennis organizations. Others are simply operated by community associations for social play, fundraisers, and so on.

The USPTA Junior Circuit format is an excellent example of community operated tournaments. The circuit offers kids valuable tournament experience locally, before they get into the higher-level USTA-sanctioned tournaments. Your community can partner with a local USPTA coach to organize the circuit. A typical circuit, with a series of tournaments running throughout the summer, is funded with affordable entry fees and sponsorships. A total circuit budget can run less than $1,200.

The Lubbock Country Club Junior Circuit in Texas, operated by Randy Mattingley, is a serious success story. The popular Lubbock Circuit (More info: lubbockcc.org) makes competitive experience accessible to Lubbock juniors. The Circuit offers kids a series of weekend tournaments all summer long for an entry fee of $12.

The bottom line is that tournament tennis offers competitive and social play opportunities for all ages and skill levels. Several types of formats, including single elimination, round robin, or compass draw tournaments, may be used to match the needs of your community.

Other Community-based Tennis Programs

There are several other programs in addition to USA Tennis Pathway:

USA School Tennis

This is a great way to introduce tennis to elementary and middle school kids in a way that fits well into their daily schedules. A fun team-based format called USA Team Tennis Ralleyball is offered either as PE Classes or after-school programs. USA School Tennis Training and incentives are available to school personnel and local tennis teachers to develop these programs. The program is free-of-charge to schools. Contact your USTA section office (More info: usta.com).

No tennis courts? No problem. The USTA can create a tennis court on any black top in minutes from its short-court net and throw-down lines of plastic. Balls and rackets are provided, too.

USA Tennis NJTL

USA Tennis NJTL (National Junior Tennis League) is a special component of USA Team Tennis (Youth). Founded by Arthur Ashe in 1969, NJTL reaches out to youngsters who may not otherwise have the opportunity to learn and play tennis.

The NJTL format has an after-school educational component, which includes mentoring, health and nutrition, college/high school preparation, tutorials, and alcohol/drug-abuse counseling. Check out Tenacity of Boston to see just how this is done (More info: tenacity.org).

Tenacity: A Story of Giving Back

Can we use tennis as a vehicle to help disadvantaged children succeed in the classroom and in life? Ned Eames and his Tenacity team hope to do just that. Each week, on three weekday afternoon dozens of Tenacity team members from its After-School Excellence Program (ASEP) fan out to various tennis facilities in the Boston area. There, the members comprising tennis instructors and volunteer academic tutors offer a unique blend of tennis instruction followed by on-site help with homework, supplementary academic teaching, and life-skill development activities.

The select group of kids enrolled in the ASEP program are middle-schools students from families with limited family resources. Organized as a partnership with "at-risk" students, parents, tennis instructors, and academic tutors, ASEP requires that students and their families make a three-year commitment to participating in all program activities while maintaining at least a B average in school (More info: Tenacity.org).

USA Wheelchair Tennis

A person with a mobility-related disability can also be part of the action. The wheelchair player can compete with other wheelchair-bound players or with able-bodied family and friends. The tennis rules are the same, except wheelchair players are allowed two bounces of the ball.

USA Special Populations Program

This program recognizes people of all ages who face all manner of challenges. The USTA supports adaptive tennis programs for those with learning disabilities, birth defects, and special emotional and at-risk needs. The USTA can help you locate grants, equipment, and resources for specially tailored programs (More info: usta.com).

Little Tennis Program

This is the most fun way to get 3 to 10-year-olds interested in tennis. Designed by the USPTA, Little Tennis (More info: littletennis.com) is touted as the tennis equivalent of little league baseball. Imagine your 3-year-old wielding a racket and smacking a large foam ball. You've got Little Tennis.

Parent-Child Program

Even well intentioned parents can, on occasion, get pushy with their kids. A parent-child round robin tournament is not only great fun for peewees but also does wonders for parents, helping them develop empathy for the pressure kids face when wins and losses are over-emphasized.

Tennis across America

Since 1990, the USPTA (More info: uspta.com) has encouraged communities across America to hold one-day events featuring free tennis clinics. Over 350 cities and 1,600 sites across America currently take advantage of this program.

Publicity for Community Tennis

Mojo promo is what you need to get the word out, although you don't want to blow your entire annual budget on a television spot. When signing Maria Sharapova is not an option, bank on cheap but effective publicity-getters.

Research by the USTA (More info: USTA Guide for Community Tennis Associations) illustrates how participants learn about USA 1-2-3 programs (Table 4.2):

Table 14.2

Flyers/Posters	33%
Word-of-mouth	29%
Local tennis pro	20%
Newspapers	10%
School/teacher	9%
Sign at location	8%
Mail	7%

Keep these survey results in mind when working with a limited budget. Here are a few ideas to reach your community inexpensively:

✓ Distribute flyers: This tried and tested method is cheap and effective. Common sense dictates posting flyers on court bulletin boards and at community centers, health clubs, sporting goods stores, pro shops, tennis clubs, youth associations, schools and colleges. The Tennis Industry Association (More info: tia.org) can help fund distribution in your area.
✓ List your events and programs with the community calendar of local newspapers and television stations.
✓ See if you can find a human-interest angle. One CTA received big-time television publicity by telling the story of a group of laid-off workers who made positive use of their free time by working to catalyze tennis in their community.
✓ As it grows, the CTA may become eligible for many community tennis awards. Win awards and let the world know you won.
✓ Develop a web site with prominent sections for upcoming events and memberships. Remember to register with leading web directories like Yahoo.

You can rig up advertising materials yourself or purchase customizable artwork from the USA Tennis Materials Catalog. Contact your USTA section office (More info: usta.com). Talk to the USPTA if you're developing promo materials for a Little Tennis program or Junior Circuit (More info: uspta.com).

Creating a Tennis Tournament

Kids love to compete, even the very young, provided the competition format is non-threatening and doesn't over-emphasize wins and loses.

If your area lacks opportunities for juniors to compete, or the competition format doesn't suit you, consider organizing your own tournament. You'll need to recruit players, interest sponsors, find courts, and get some mojo publicity. This can all be fairly easy if it's a small tournament.

Players

You can find eager participants at schools with tennis programs, clinics conducted by local pros, and nearby tennis clubs. Tournaments can be run with any multiple of two players. It's more interesting, though, when you have two groups at different skill levels with eight players in each group. The maximum number of players is 32. A new director may find numbers beyond that get unwieldy. If you have an odd number of players, fill the draw with byes and award those byes to seeded players, such as top-ranked juniors from the area.

Format

Choose a format appropriate for the skill level of registrants. When working with peewees with less than a year of tennis under their belts, consider using half-courts and foam balls, or multi-colored pressure-less balls.

A round robin format is preferable because each player gets to play every other player at the same level. This format is less threatening than the elimination format in which a player drops from the tournament as soon as he loses a match. Round robins can be singles, doubles, and parent-child play.

Emphasize the fun factor. Award not only the winner, but also the player who exhibited the best sportsmanship throughout the tournament, the most improved player, and the kid who chased down every ball. Hold an end-of-day carnival event where everyone is welcome. Distribute party favors to all competitors, event participants, and volunteers!

Giving Back

Jennifer Pitzen, an experienced tournament director, runs the USTA Girls 18 Super National Hard Court Championships. With over 132 competitors, managing transportation, accommodations, and play can be quite a challenge. Still, Jennifer incorporates a Kid's Day into the program and introduces over 100 inner city children to this wonderful sport.

A few hours of clean up a court that needs one or honoring a local pro are examples of giving-back that could be incorporated as part of the tournament. It's great education for the kids and helps them see beyond wins and losses.

As you gain experience at local tournaments, you might want to try holding a USTA-sanctioned event for juniors. Follow up success there with USTA satellite and challenger tournaments. Who knows? You might one day reach the pinnacle of tournament directing by hosting an ATP or WTA event in your town.

Tennis Software to the Rescue

Today is tournament day. The draw sheet has 48 kids at 3 different skill levels. Two kids reported sick and three say they ought to be playing at a different level. Little Karrina is wondering how she got put in the Boys 10s. As a tournament director, you've got to straighten out the draw sheet quickly. You can scratch your head and choose to do it yourself, or let a computer equipped with tennis software do the scratching for you.

Welcome to tournament management software. These systems can create and revise draws on the fly. Just type in or revise the names, skill-levels, number of courts and rounds and the system does the rest, including printing out a complete new line-up and court assignments. GamePlan software is one such affordable solution. Best suited for small tournaments, the software is available for under $50.

As your CTA grows, tournaments can get fancier. You may want the system to handle compass and first-round consolation, in addition to elimination and round robin. The tournament may be held at multiple sites simultaneously. The Tournament Management Systems (TMS) software can coordinate multi-sites and more, but can also get pricey as you pile on features. In addition to making draws, TMS allows a referee to record results, submit these results to the sanctioning office, and publish them.

Fortunately, if you're holding a USTA-sanctioned tournament or running a USA Tennis Pathway program, you can avoid buying software. The USTA makes event management services available to you. Many activities such as tournament announcement and player and team registrations are handled through TennisLink, the USTA's online system (More info: usta.com). For other functions, the USTA offers the tournament site a license.

Building A Junior Tennis Business

If you're the entrepreneurial sort or want to make profitable use of free time, consider starting a business delivering tennis programs to kids. Frankly, one could find other, more profitable avenues of pursuit. But if you love tennis, a junior tennis business will yield profits beyond those reflected on the balance sheet.

Silicon Valley, the capital of high-tech entrepreneurialism, is high strung and exciting. Notwithstanding the dot-com crash, recent college grads and seasoned entrepreneurs still engage in nerf gun battles and work through the night. These overachievers are known for building stuff in their garages and turning it into something millions use worldwide. Think what could happen if just a portion of that fervor was directed to tennis.

The great Bollettieris and IMGs are in the business of creating and maintaining sports champions, but the under-served markets are at the grass roots level: the business of developing millions of recreational players; the business of transforming french-fry logged, obese kids into toned tennis enthusiasts. Developing recreational players can be both a passionate experience and a great business opportunity.

The Valley teaches us two rules of entrepreneurial wisdom:

- ✓ Think big. Start small.
- ✓ Lone rangers go nowhere.

A parent, a coach, and an MBA can pool their talents to build a viable tennis business for your community. Fortunately, there's a wonderful support system for tennis programming, the highly successful USA Tennis Pathway program (More info: usta.com). Look at it this way. There's an untapped market and lots of infrastructure support from the USTA and allied organizations. All that's needed is American free enterprise to serve up a winner.

15

Inside Tennis Organizations

"People understand contests. You take a bunch of kids throwing rocks at random and people look askance, but if you go and hold a rock-throwing contest – people understand that."
DON MURRAY, football coach.

People, organizations, and money, in that order, make the tennis world go round. When we, as parents and coaches, understand their roles and motivations, we're in a better position to help our kids develop a roadmap for their future. Knowing how the system works makes our own contributions to the tennis world more effective.

Here then is the inside skinny on tennis organizations, ordered in the way a parent and kid may encounter them.

USTA

If there's one organization a parent or coach raising a tennis kid should support, this is it. Founded in 1881, the United States Tennis Association (More info: usta.com) is a volunteer-based organization with nearly 665,000 individual members and 7,000 organizational members. As the national governing body for tennis, the USTA uses its nearly $180 million annual budget to promote and develop the growth of tennis, from the community level to the professional game.

The USTA and You

Who contributes to the annual budget? Consider this, over 100 million television viewers and nearly 660,000 ticket holders took in the US Open in 2005. If you were one of them, guess what, *you* contributed to the USTA coffers. Yep, this tournament alone generates over 80 percent of the USTA's annual revenue.

As the owner of the US Open, the USTA affords its members the opportunity to get the best seats and discount travel packages to this and many other tournaments. There are other important membership benefits, especially for a parent.

By joining the USTA, you and your child automatically become members of one of the seventeen sectional associations throughout the country. This puts you in contact with the entire tennis playing community in your area and provides access to USA League tennis and USTA-sanctioned tournaments.

Annual membership in the USTA costs $15 for a junior and $55 for the entire family. Membership includes subscriptions to the excellent Tennis magazine and USTA national and sectional magazines. Your support helps USTA bring tennis to wheelchair athletes, people with developmental disabilities, and underprivileged kids.

There are opportunities to connect with the USTA other than membership. Volunteer at your local USTA member organization. Serve on local and national USTA committees. Speak up and set the course for the future of tennis. Bottom-line: get involved. You owe it to all the tennis kids out there.

Organization

Promoting tennis to a nationwide population of some 290 million people and serving the needs of 24 million tennis players require the effort of many individuals and organizations.

The USTA operates through seventeen geographical sections. Each section maintains its own full-time staff to administer USTA programs, establishes its own tournament schedule, and issues its own rankings. Twelve of these sections are further divided into districts. All of these sections and districts have community tennis associations (CTAs) that are a vital part of the grassroots delivery system.

A 15-member board of directors guides the USTA. Each member is elected for a two-year term. In addition, three major councils, served by volunteer committees, oversee particular aspects of the USTA's work: community players, competitive players, and professional players. A paid workforce at the organization's headquarters in White Plains, New York effects national coordination and administration.

Professional Tournaments

In keeping with its reputation as the largest and most successful tennis tournament in the world, the US Open brings in $152 million, a heck of a lot more than the $16 million it hands out as prize money and making it the USTA's chief cash cow.

Year-round, the USTA runs a variety of other professional tournaments, including:

- US Men's Clay Court Championships – one of the oldest continuing events, dating back to 1910; currently held at the Westside Tennis Club in Houston, Texas.
- US Women's Hard Court Championships – more commonly known as Pilot Pen Tennis; one of the oldest women-only events in the country, dating back to 1948; currently held in New Haven, Connecticut.
- USTA Professional Circuits – the world's premier developmental circuit for aspiring professional tennis players. It allows players to gain the experience and ranking points needed to participate on the major pro tours and in Grand Slam tournaments. There are three levels of tournaments: Satellites, Futures, and Challengers. The tour consists of nearly 100 tournaments coast-to-coast and disburses more than $3 million in prize money.

Amateur Competition

The USTA supports national teams at the Davis Cup, Fed Cup, and the Olympics. For the rest of us, well, there are hundreds of USTA-sanctioned competition opportunities.

The USA League Tennis (Adult) is for competitive teams. Players face-off against opponents at the same level. The USTA recognizes six NTRP levels from 2.5 to 5.0. Each level leads up to a national championship held September to October. The league attracts nearly 490,00 participants. And how's this for an official statistic: National championship participants consume over 5,760 bananas! Now we know the secret of that fluid split-step volley.

The USTA, with its section and district offices, interacts with and offers support to thousands of high schools tennis teams. The state athletic associations operate competitions for high schools.

A competitive junior's primary focus will probably be the USA Tournament Tennis program. Several types of formats, including single elimination, round robin, or compass draw tournaments, are sanctioned by the USTA all over the country. The USTA also offers specialized coaching to top-ranked juniors.

USA Tennis

While professional tennis brings in the dough, fan support and growth of tennis is ensured at the community level. USA Tennis Pathway, spearheaded by the USTA, is designed to do just that.

USA Tennis 1-2-3 and USA Team Tennis are two programs of Pathway, through which a new player at any age level can learn tennis in a relaxed recreational setting. USA Tennis 1-2-3 is a series of six introductory low-cost group lessons, while Team Tennis offers kids and adults the opportunity to play organized matches in a fun, friendly atmosphere. The USA Tennis National Junior Tennis League (NJTL) reaches out to at-risk kids with a mix of team tennis and education.

Started in 1998, with $50-million and a five-year goal to increase tennis participants by 800,000, Pathway has been wildly successful. The program reached its goal three and a half years into the initiative.

USPTA & PTR

Each summer community centers in the San Francisco Bay Area conduct weeklong tennis camps for kids. Camp instructors include both certified pros and college players from the community. By the second or third day, there is usually a striking difference between kids taught by a certified pro and those under the direction of a college player.

The certified pro uses seemingly spontaneous drills to hold the kids' attention and create an almost rhythmic improvement in technique among the members of his class. While the college player may possess excellent skills, his students don't assimilate techniques as easily. A college player often wastes a lot of time trying to handle the easily distracted kids.

There are two excellent institutions for certifying tennis professionals – the United States Professional Tennis Association (USPTA) and the Professional Tennis Registry (PTR).

USPTA

Founded in 1927, the USPTA (More info: uspta.com) is an association of teaching professionals with over 12,500 members. Headquartered in Houston, Texas, the organization has 17 regional divisions.

USPTA offers two membership options. The first is a professional, career-path certification designed for full-time tennis teachers. Certification is available in three levels depending upon number of years of teaching experience – Pro 3, 2 and 1, with level 1 reflecting the greatest amount of experience. The USPTA has specialization paths for professionals who have attained Pro 1 level –

Competitive Player Development, Little Tennis, Facility Management, and so on.

The USPTA Developmental Coach is the second certification option. This is a non-career-path category for people who teach part time or coach high school teams. All USPTA members receive $9 million in on-court liability insurance, subscriptions to Tennis and Tennis Week magazines, and an online listing so players and potential employers can find them.

In addition to education, the USPTA designs programs like Tennis Across America, Little Tennis, Junior Circuit, and Adult Leagues. Unlike the USA Tennis programs supported by the USTA, these are run independently by your local certified professional.

PTR

For all practical purposes, the PTR (More info: ptrtennis.org) is identical in its role to the USPTA. The Registry runs continuing education workshops, issues certifications, and offers similar benefits to members – liability insurance, magazine subscriptions, and online listing.

The PTR offers an education based on a standardized method designed by a remarkable coach and PTR founder – Dennis Van der Meer. The application and annual dues are about half of those for the USPTA. Members are certified as Associate Instructor, Instructor, or Professional. The Registry boasts a membership of over 10,300.

NRPA

The National Recreation and Park Association (NRPA. More info: nrpa.org) is the nation's largest independent, non-profit public service organization advocating quality recreation, parks, and environmental conservation efforts.

As a membership organization, the NRPA relies upon the active involvement of both citizen and professional members to achieve the broad vision and mission of the association. Various membership categories are available including Student, Citizen, Board Member, and Agency memberships for groups.

A Board of Trustees and a National Forum comprised of citizens and professionals govern the NRPA. The Board of Trustees sets policy and the National Forum develops programs. Vision 2010 is an action plan developed by the NRPA that counts expansion of citizen representation in its National Forum as a top goal.

The NRPA works closely with the USTA in running USA Tennis programs at public parks. NRPA members can also take advantage of a discounted license for World Team Tennis (WTT). The NRPA publication – Park, Recreation, Open Space and Greenway Guidelines – is a great resource for need assessment and the planning of community tennis courts.

IHRSA

Over 33 million Americans pump up, rally, tee off, and lap their way to good health at 18,200 health clubs. Those numbers are good enough to sprout an association. The International Health, Racquet & Sportsclub Association (IHRSA. More info: ihrsa.org) is a not-for-profit trade association representing privately owned health and fitness facilities, gyms, spas, sports clubs and their suppliers worldwide.

Headquartered in Boston, IHRSA has over 6,500 member clubs and publishes research findings related to the club market. An IHRSA survey of member clubs shows tennis ranked in the top 5 among profitable programs for health clubs.

NIRSA

Getting college students to try, learn, and play tennis is an important component of the USA Pathway Program. The USTA partners with the Intercollegiate Tennis Association (ITA. More info: itatennis.com) and National Intramural-Recreational Sports Association (NIRSA. More info: nirsa.org) to run USA 1-2-3 and USA Team Tennis programs on college campuses. NIRSA is a non-profit association of nearly 4,000 recreational sports professionals representing 700-plus colleges and universities, military bases, and other institutions.

Tennis Industry Association

Guess who's most happy when rackets, balls, and other tennis paraphernalia fly off pro shop shelves? The manufacturers and the Tennis Industry Association, of course (TIA. More info: tennisindustry.org).

Participating Partners

The TIA is a trade association comprised of tennis companies involved in the manufacturing, marketing, and sales of tennis products, together with tennis publications, tennis management firms, and other allied organizations. The Board of Directors is a Who's Who of power brokers in the tennis industry – Nike, Wilson, HEAD/Penn, K-Swiss, USTA, USPTA, and Tennis magazine, to name a few.

What's striking about the TIA is not only its recognition that developing tennis-loving communities is good for its members' bottom lines, but the fact that the association puts its money where its mouth is.

Take for instance their Participating Partners program. The 15 or so member companies contribute a percentage of their product sales to a fund that is deployed to execute a suite of well thought out community-based programs designed to grow the game. The community develops new and more accomplished players and the manufacturers sell more rackets – lots of them. It's a win-win program, not just on paper, but in action, too.

Community Programs

The TIA is a top financial contributor to the highly successful USA Tennis program spearheaded by the USTA. The TIA/USTA team is at work again in the Growing Tennis 50/50 program. This time the TIA is taking the lead in running the program, with matching funds from the USTA. Growing Tennis 50/50 is a program that offers funding to any tennis facility that aims to introduce new adult players. The TIA matches 50 percent of the promotional dollars budgeted for this purpose by a participating facility.

Scooby Doo, where are you? The Cartoon Network Tennis Club operated by the TIA delivers a promotional kit at a subsidized cost to any club or program promoting tennis. The kit includes a court banner, poster, sales flyers, newspaper ad slicks, and a Scooby Doo stand-up, guaranteed to get little ones in the game!

NFHS

The principals, superintendents, and school boards of most high schools and junior high schools in United States are members of their state's school athletic association. The association, also called a federation, sets rules for high school athletics in individual states, controls athlete recruitment, holds championships, and so on. The New York State Public High School Athletic Association (NYSPHSAA. More info: nysphsaa.org) and the California Interscholastic Federation (CIF. More info: cifstate.org) are two examples.

State school athletic associations in turn are members of a national organization called the National Federation of State High School Associations (NFHS. More info: nfhs.org). The NFHS provides leadership and national coordination for state school athletic associations. The NFHS publishes reports on sports safety issues and a survey that tracks participation levels in various school sports.

Tennis Academies

There are certain academies that have long since graduated from being specialized college-preparatory schools for tennis kids to legendary institutions that control the destiny of tennis, not just today, but tennis 10 to 15 years from now. Nick Bollettieri (More info: imgacademies.com), Harry Hopman (More info: saddlebrooksports.com), Dennis Van der Meer (More info: vandermeertennis.com), and Rick Macci (More info: rickmacci.com) are just a few.

Remarkably, many of these institutions have resisted the urge to rest on their laurels. Instead, they look forward by bringing in new management, introducing cutting-edge techniques, and expanding programs. The academies continue to do well, producing tennis champions as well as good college graduates.

Don't expect to have these tennis masters greet your kid personally when he arrives at the academy. All of these famous examples of American enterprise have lent years to their institutions, handing down systems, techniques, and guidelines. Academy instructors use those systems and techniques and follow those guidelines to reflect the master's way.

For example, at Bollettieri's each coach participates in a cutting-edge, one-year coaching certification program and is then re-certified every 12 months as part of a continuing education program. Dennis Van der Meer maintains that his method is "teacher proof" – simple enough to be taught even by a novice instructor.

As a kid develops competitive ability, parents often have to make a choice between tournament preparation and the rigors of a public school schedule. Tennis academies are a great solution, with school schedules woven around tennis training.

The convenience of a proven system, well-trained coaches, and topnotch facilities comes with a steep price. At Bollettieri's, full-time students pay a minimum of $30,000-plus annually for tennis instruction, boarding, and tournament expenses. School tuition costs over $11,000 and fees can climb dramatically for tournament travel and special coaching for higher levels of competition. A few academy scholarships are available.

In addition to full-time programs, virtually all tennis academies offer part-time programs and camps for juniors and adults, including professional athletes and corporate groups. By reaching out to players at all levels these tennis institutions have proven yet again the merits of individual enterprise, consistently turning out college athletic scholarship winners, physically fit people, tennis professionals, and champions.

NCAA

The National Collegiate Athletic Association (NCAA. More info: ncaa.org) is an organization of nearly 980 schools charged with setting rules for academic eligibility and scholarships for college-bound athletes. The NCAA also enforces regulations regarding amateur status and drug testing at championship games.

Divisions

Schools are classified into three divisions based on how many sports they offer and the availability of athletic scholarships. Division I schools must offer seven sports for both men and women and meet minimum financial aid award requirements for their athletic programs. Division II schools offer four sports and student-athletes generally pay for college through a combination of scholarship money, grants, student loans, and employment earnings. A Division III school does not provide athletic scholarships but runs five or more sports. Division I has about 320 schools, Division II has 260, and Division III has 400.

Given the size of athletic budgets, the very best coaches and college players participate in Division I. Consequently, the best college teams are also in Division I. The best teams in Divisions II and III hold their own, though, when they compete against Division I schools at the NCAA Championships. A school's so-called reputation has no bearing on divisional classification. Harvard is in Division I, whereas MIT is a Division III school.

The number of schools offering tennis programs is higher than those offering football and equal to those that offer basketball and soccer. Men's tennis is available at nearly 770 of the 980 NCAA schools and women's tennis is offered at even more, some 900 schools. Tennis athletes number almost 15,500 men and women.

Operations

The NCAA holds 87 championship games in 22 sports, including tennis. Television rights to these championships are a very big deal, generating 80 percent of the NCAA's $340 million in annual revenues. Seventy percent of the championship money is put back into Division I grants-in-aid, coaching salaries, and administration.

The 14-member executive committee, comprising school heads – 10 from Division I and 2 each representing Divisions II & III – is the driving force behind NCAA operations. Then there are the inescapable sports and rules committees.

The NCAA has separate sports committees for men's and women's tennis but works closely with a specialized organization called the Intercollegiate Tennis Association (ITA. More info: itatennis.com) to set rules. The ITA is also entrusted with collegiate rankings and holding all intercollegiate regional tournaments.

The NCAA tennis committee uses the ITA rankings to select teams for the NCAA Championships in May. The traditional bonus for the NCAA singles and doubles champions is a wild card entry to the US Open.

NAIA

The National Association of Intercollegiate Athletics (NAIA. More info: naia.org) is the second-largest association, after the NCAA, of fully accredited four-year colleges. Like the NCAA, the NAIA sets eligibility rules for athletes attending one of the 400 member colleges. There are nearly 180 men's tennis programs and 190 for women, with five scholarships in each program. The NAIA also works with the ITA to set rules for tennis and hold championships. Unlike the NCAA, recruitment to NAIA colleges has fewer restrictions and there is no clearinghouse.

NJCAA

Junior colleges offer opportunities for players who are not sure whether they want to attend a four-year school. Many student-athletes want to experience professional tennis as soon as possible; other college players eventually transfer to four-year schools.

The National Junior College Athletic Association (NJCAA. More info: njcaa.org) boasts a membership of 530 two-year institutions participating in 15 sports. NJCAA members run hundreds of tennis programs and work with the ITA to set rules of the game and hold intercollegiate competitions.

ITA

Comprised of nearly 1,500 men's and women's coaches, the Intercollegiate Tennis Association (ITA. More info: itatennis.com) represents over 1,200 colleges from all NCAA Divisions, the NAIA, and all junior and community colleges.

The ITA administers rankings for all collegiate tennis and runs regional and national tournaments. The ITA epitomizes private enterprise: membership dues and corporate sponsors fund the entire annual budget.

Tournaments

The Association holds over 80 Division I and Small College Regional Championships, the National Intercollegiate Indoor Championships, National Small College Championships, and National Team Indoor Championships. Based on the rankings accrued in these tournaments and other team matches, the NCAA selects teams for the NCAA Championship held in May of each year.

The ITA also works closely with the USTA to run a summer circuit with regional tournaments leading up to the ITA National Summer Championships. The summer circuit is open to junior players, college players, and college graduates. The only requirements are USTA membership and amateur status.

In order to increase tennis awareness in colleges, the ITA, USTA, and NIRSA (National Intramural-Recreational Sports Association) collaborate to introduce the USA Team Tennis on Campus program.

ITF

"Edwards Nets…Tried & Tested." This has been the motto of the .UK-based tennis net manufacturer since 1884. You can find them at Grand Slams and neighborhood courts throughout the world, surviving the Arizona sun, Caribbean hurricanes, and a professional player's whiplash. You can use all the same epithets to describe the International Tennis Federation, an institution with English roots that has steadfastly withstood many rough challenges to its existence and authority (ITF. More info: itftennis.com).

History

The ITF has been the governing body of world tennis since 1913. In the early years when tennis was pure recreation, the ITF exerted tremendous control over the game and its tournaments. An entire new industry called professional tennis was born in 1968. The players formed their own association (ATP) and began operating prize-money tournaments.

The ITF initially opposed professional tennis. With time, the two bodies reconciled and divvied up control of different facets of the game. The ITF is now responsible for the Rules of Tennis, including specifications for courts, rackets and balls, and officiating. The ITF also enforces a joint anti-doping program.

In addition, the ITF owns the international team sports events, Davis Cup for men and Fed Cup for women. The ITF is also an affiliate of the International Olympic Committee.

Organization

Today, the ITF is an umbrella organization with 199 national associations and six regional associations. A 12-member Board of Directors, chaired by the president, is elected every two years. The Board is composed of candidates nominated by national associations.

Junior Competition

With assistance from the regional associations, the ITF has created a worldwide structure of international junior team and individual events, from 14s to 18s. The goal is to prepare juniors for professional play. Lleyton Hewitt honed his skills at an ITF boy's event in 1995 before turning pro and eventually reaching the Number 1 spot.

Players competing in the 18s attain a junior world ranking for singles and doubles. To be eligible for a year-end ranking, players are required to compete in six events, three of which must be foreign and three of which must be of a certain Group A status (More info: itfjuniors.com).

The ITF also operates four junior World Team Championships: the World Junior Tennis (14s), Junior Davis Cup (Boys), Junior Fed Cup (Girls), and ITF junior team competition (18s).

So, the next time you see professional officiator, Mike Morrisey, hanging out at the US Open, or a new larger-than-normal regulation ball, or a bunch of kids in Davis Cup uniforms at an airport, think ITF.

WTA

"Battle of the sexes. On court. For prize money." Headlines hot enough to make a tabloid fly off newsstands. But this one's for real and reflects the disparity in prize money between men and women, even though female players put in equal work and often receive better television ratings.

Equal Pay

It's understandably frustrating that in 2002, 37th-ranked Arnaud Clement made more than 15th-ranked Patty Schnyder did. Ask Pam Shriver, the tennis hall of famer. Shriver has taken every opportunity to speak out against the inequality – on television, in the papers, and much to the chagrin of the official facing her, in person.

Thanks to Pam Shriver and others like her, the tennis establishment is beginning to see the light. The US Open and Australian Open now have equal prize money for men and women winners.

The English and French are inching closer to parity, though they're not equal yet. Women players are doing what's smart, accepting improved parity in prize money for now, signing on the dotted line, and continuing to fight for even better rewards.

When all is said and done, women's tennis has come a long way since the Pacific Southwest tournament in 1970 when tournament director, Jack Kramer, refused to amend the purse: $12,500 for the men, $1,500 for the women. As a result, Billie Jean King and company broke away from the tennis establishment to form a tour of their own, the Virginia Slims.

By 1971, a three-tournament circuit in 1970 had grown to 19 tournaments. Since then, women's tennis has gone from strength to strength. Aside from a new name, the Women's Tennis Association (WTA. More info: wtatour.com), the tour now boasts 60-plus tournaments in over 30 countries and prize money totaling more than $52 million. And so the princess kissed the toad!

The Board

The WTA Tour is registered as a non-profit corporation headquartered in St Petersburg, Florida. Its members are the players, its tournaments, and the ITF.

The WTA Board of Directors meld the sports and business aspects of the game with three player representatives, three tournament directors, one ITF representative, two non-affiliated directors, and the CEO.

Tournaments

The WTA tour is comprised of the Tour Championships, four Grand Slam events, and 60-plus Tier events. A Tier 1 tournament offers minimum prize money of over $1.26 million. The money scales down for each tier, to $110,000 for a Tier 5 event.

In addition to prize money, the winner takes home computer ranking points, again earned on a sliding scale from a minimum of 275 points for tier 1 to a meager 80 points at the lowest rung. Court surfaces are evenly divided between hard courts and red clay courts. A player has to perform well on both surfaces to earn good computer rankings.

Over 50 percent of the tournaments require travel to Europe, with only a dozen Tier events taking place in the United States. Players circumvent the globe many times before the season ends.

Commitment

The sport of tennis and the business of tennis play the dating game. As long as the dating game takes place on an even playing field, the relationship thrives. Translation: so long as stadium turnstiles click and television ratings soar, everybody's happy. But when one partner begins to dominate, the relationship sours and tennis fans are turned off.

The Player Commitment Lists developed by the WTA exemplify this relationship. A pool of 20 players drawn from the top 16 computer-ranked singles players and 4 wild cards make up one such commitment list called the Gold List. Each player in the Gold List is then ranked based on marketability.

The marketing folks refer to them as players who "move products." For example, a player placing 10th in the computer rankings may be ranked 3rd on the Gold List, simply because people believe she is more marketable. As you can see, the Gold List ranking is highly subjective. A pro player may not be anywhere near the top 20 in computer rankings, but she can get wild-carded and be given a high rank on the Gold List because the WTA believes she can put fannies in the seats.

For players, a high ranking on the Gold List means more opportunities to compete at top-tier events and fatter year-end bonuses.

For tournament directors, it's a commitment from the WTA that a minimum number of Gold List players will play in their events.

Mentoring

In the early 90s, Jennifer Capriati, who turned pro at 14, lost her tennis groove amid a swelter of personal and drug problems. She disappeared from the WTA for two-and-a-half years, away from the high-intensity glare of the professional game.

The WTA responded by crafting two brilliant policies: an age eligibility rule and a mentoring program. A player under 14 years of age is no longer allowed to play in the WTA. After age 14, players are phased-up by limiting them to just a few tournaments the first year. More tournaments are added each year until the player reaches age 18, when all age restrictions are removed.

The mentoring program pairs teenage players with former pros, who, unlike parent-coaches, know the rigors of the circuit firsthand. The Venus Williams-Pam Shriver pairing is a famous example. Mentors and protégés work together for 24 months via phone, email, and in-person sessions.

You have indeed come a long way, baby.

ATP

Hamilton Jordan, White House chief of staff during the Jimmy Carter presidency, has always been a man of causes, be it fighting discrimination in the civil rights era, volunteering for the war in Vietnam, spearheading Carter's campaign victory, negotiating the Iran hostage crisis, or surviving three bouts of cancer. Jordan's warrior qualities were desperately needed in 1989 when the Association of Tennis Professionals (ATP. More info: atptennis.com), a players' union, decided to rebel against the Men's Tennis Council in order to have a greater say in how the men's game was run.

That year, the association, led by executive director Jordan, took over control of the men's worldwide circuit, with the exception of the Grand Slams. Soon the association matured from a vigilante union to a partnership of players and tournament directors, each with an equal voice in managing the circuit. The name was shortened to ATP.

Balance

The ATP reflects its union roots in its Board, with three player representatives, three tournament representatives, and the CEO. The

Board gets its input from two councils elected by two ATP members, the Player Council and the Tournament Council.

Recently, the ATP added an Advisory Council comprised of a select group of global leaders who will combine their interest in tennis with insight and advice on business strategies.

The ATP headquarters is located in beautiful Pointe Vedra, Florida. The headquarters epitomize a fair and balanced organization, right down to the tennis courts located on the premises. There are 11 courts, with a good distribution of hard, clay, and grass surfaces.

Membership

A tennis player has one way to gain access to ATP membership – hit the ball and hit it hard. The top 200 ranked in singles or 100 ranked in doubles get in Division I, with benefits ranging from the down-to-earth health insurance and travel discounts to the more upscale – trainers and masseuses. Up to 500 ranked in singles, or 250 in doubles, players are bunched in lower Division II. The rest of us, well, we get the bleachers and the really lucky ones are boxed!

While the tour makes 70-odd tournament hops across 6 continents, the 4 Grand Slams, 9 Masters Series and end-of-year Tennis Masters Cup events are where the stars congregate and the stakes are high.

To determine eligibility, the ATP uses two cleverly designed ranking systems – the ATP Entry and the Champions Race. Both are mathematical methods and computer-calculated. Translation: No tournament can keep you out simply because they don't like your spiked hair. They *could* keep you out of a match, though, if you show up in a sleeveless shirt. But that's beside the point.

Rank and Pile

The ATP Entry rank determines qualification for entry and seeding at most tournaments. The rank is based on points earned in a tournament. There are two types of points a player can earn – Round points and Bonus points.

Round points are earned by advancing through the different rounds of a tournament. Blokes who lose in the first round of a Tennis Masters Series go home with 5 points, while the winner of the tournament earns 500. The points vary depending upon the prize money.

Bonus points are awarded for winning against high-ranked players. Beat the Number 1, pile on 50 bonus points. The bonus points scale down until you reach the single point earned for beating a player ranked between 150 and 200.

Now comes the fun part, ranking. The number crunchers at ATP don't just total the points and declare the player with the highest number of points Number 1. That way a rookie could play every tournament, accumulating points little by little, and attain an artificially high ranking – for a while anyway, until he passes out from sheer exhaustion.

The ATP Entry System adds up the points from the four Grand Slams, the nine Tennis Masters series and the Tennis Masters Cup, together with the best five results from all eligible tournaments in the Entry System period. In most cases, the Entry System period is the past 52-weeks.

When a player is ineligible to play one of the 13 majors by virtue of a low rank, the number of other eligible tournaments is increased by one and so on. However, if a player who is eligible to compete in any of the majors did not play, tough luck. He would still be considered as having participated and allocated big-o-bagel points. This somewhat brutal rule is designed to ensure star turnout at elite tournaments.

The Champions Race

While the ATP Entry System is a rolling system indicative of performance in the last 12 months, the Champions Race is calendar-based. Every player starts at zero in January.

The Champions Race System has a separate points table, but allocation works like the ATP Entry System. By years end the top seven players in the Champions Race qualify to duke it out for the Tennis Masters Cup. The eighth place will go to the highest-placed Grand Slam champion who finishes ranked between 8th and 20th.

The tournament starts as a round robin with the four best players slugging it out in elimination rounds for a major share of the $3.7 million prize money.

The player who earns the most Race points in a calendar year is the World Number 1. The Top 50 in the Race also earn a handsome Christmas bonus. The ATP says it designed the Champions Race to build rivalries and showcase the best players at elite events.

WTT

Billie Jean King wants to prove tennis can be an adult, co-ed team sport. World Team Tennis (WTT. More info: wtt.com), founded by King, does it with a unique format. Each team is comprised of two men, two women, and a coach. Team matches consist of five events of one set each: men's singles, women's singles, men's doubles, women's doubles, and mixed doubles. The first team to win five games wins the set. One point is awarded for each game won.

The WTT got a shot in the arm when Andre Agassi signed on with the Sacramento Capitals. The WTT professional league currently has ten teams participating. Matches are played in July and the top teams face off at the USTA National Tennis Center in Flushing Meadows in August.

The organization also runs a year-round recreation league using the same format leading up to the WTT National Championships. WTT has great appeal for players interested in a social setting.

Grand Slams

The Grand Slams are the cream of sporting events, humongously popular with fat prize monies and behemoth egos on the line. Television networks trip over each other to win broadcast rights to these events and star players don't need to be required to play at the Slams, they actually want to.

A recent economic impact study conducted by the Sports Management Research Institute (SMRI) estimates that the US Open alone generates over $420 million in direct revenue for the neighboring tri-state area, more than any other annual sports or entertainment event in the United States.

Given the glare of publicity that surrounds the four Grand Slam events – the Australian Open (More info: ausopen.org), the Wimbledon Championships (More info: wimbledon.org), the French Open (More info: rolandgarros.com) and the US Open (More info: usopen.org), we know a lot about them.

Junior Championships

We know, of course, that the Australian and US Opens are played on rubberized hard courts. Wimbledon is played on grass and the French Open on red clay. We are aware that each is among the richest professional events in its part of the world. We may also know that these events have the largest number of entrants of all tennis tournaments, with a draw size of 128.

What may not be apparent is that away from grandstands, sprinkled on remote, outlying courts where the Junior Championships are held, blood is often drawn. No one worked harder than Ryan Henry in the 2002 Junior Wimbledon for 18s. The young Australian played a record-breaking, marathon third set against Clement Morel. The match stretched over three rain-delayed days and a record 75 games. There are no tiebreakers in Junior Wimbledon. Ryan eventually won the epic third-round match 7-5, 6-7, 26-24.

Family Doubles

When Sandon Stolle and partner, Cyril Suk, won the doubles title at the 1998 US Open, defeating Mark Knowles and Daniel Nestor, Stolle and his father, Fred, became the only father and son to win a US doubles championship. Fred Stolle was also a three-time US doubles titlist.

Qualifiers

A week before the first round of the main draw, 128 hopefuls, called qualifiers, descend on the Grand Slam venue. The top 16 from the qualifying tournament will gain entry to the main draw. However, even a first round loser, if participating as a professional, can make $3,000, perhaps enough to pay for her plane fare and meals.

In the early rounds of the main draw many of the top 16 qualifiers, unfortunately, end up as road-kill for the other 112 ranked or wild-card players. All the same, early rounds can produce the gems of the tournament as a gutsy qualifier stretches the match as long as she can, gaining valuable experience and ranking points.

The national tennis federations independently own each Grand Slam event. For instance, Tennis Australia owns the Australian Open. In 1989, the Grand Slams joined forces for the first time to form the Grand Slam Committee to administer Grand Slam rules. The Grand Slams are open to both amateurs and professionals.

International Tennis Hall of Fame

Casino and Tennis – a fortuitous mix found only in Las Vegas, coincidentally the original hometown of Andre Agassi. However, there's a certain "casino" of an entirely different character on the opposite coast. In fact, the Newport Casino in Rhode Island derives its name from "casina," an Italian word for "little house," and sports immaculate lawn tennis courts and a stately museum – the International Tennis Hall of Fame (More info: tennisfame.com).

The Newport Casino, site of the first US National Championships in 1881, was officially sanctioned as a Hall of Fame institution by the United States Tennis Association in 1954 and was recognized by the International Tennis Federation in 1986. The Hall of Fame is dedicated to preserving the history of the game, inspiring the next generation, enshrining tennis greats, and providing a landmark destination for tennis fans worldwide.

Players are elected to the Hall of Fame primarily on the basis of their competitive record. Boris Becker, Pam Shriver, and Mats Wilander are a few of the recent additions to this elite club. The Enshrinement Gallery pays tribute to each Hall of Famer with a plaque commemorating their illustrious careers. Strolling through the gallery, you might catch yourself observing a little one gazing up at the plaques. You wonder – is he the next Rod "Rocket" Laver?

16

Movers and Shakers

"I am tired of hearing about money, money, money, money, money. I just want to play the game, drink Pepsi, wear Reebok."
SHAQUILLE O'NEAL, professional basketball player.

Two or three decades ago you could have counted on the fingers of one hand the number of companies in the business of marketing and managing sports. Today there are hundreds of medium to large-sized corporations and thousands of one-person armies in this line of work, all making up a multi-billion dollar industry. At the center of the sports business are three functions: athlete representation, the marketing of specific sports, and marketing companies that utilize sports and sports personalities.

Sports Marketing Companies

Mark McCormack invented sports marketing. If you think you're not acquainted with his work, then you've never watched television coverage of Wimbledon, never attended a WTA tournament, and have never heard of Lindsay Davenport and the Bollettieri Academy. Let's just say this: McCormack made it his life's work to connect these dots and more, growing one of the largest sports marketing organizations in the world.

IMG

After graduating from Yale, Mark McCormack spent several years with a Cleveland law firm and then hung out his own shingle in 1959. About that time, a young professional golfer walked through his door. His name was Arnold Palmer. McCormack was soon getting his new client lucrative exhibition and endorsement deals. Before long more young golfers stopped by.

Business was lucrative and McCormick decided to devote himself full-time to managing the careers of his clients, increasing their earnings through exhibitions, endorsements, advertising gigs, and tournament appearance fees. Along the way he set up the International Management Group (IMG. More info: imgworld.com) and sports marketing was born.

Convinced of a coming boom, McCormack moved into tennis, signing Rod Laver and other stalwarts of the era. Instead of merely supplying players, he began to support the tours financially, offering a multimillion-dollar guarantee to the ATP Men's Tour and Women's Tennis Council. At the same time, he was buying tournaments in various cities.

A few years later, IMG bought the Bollettieri Tennis Academy, transforming it into a 200-acre multi-sport facility for 550 full-time students and 10,000 part-timers. Meanwhile, Trans World International, the television arm of IMG, began producing thousands of hours of sports programming, including Wimbledon and the Olympics. Essentially, IMG creates players and represents them, creates events and broadcasts them.

IMG represents many top-ranked players, including the Williams sisters, Jennifer Capriati, Lindsay Davenport, Monica Seles, Tommy Haas, and Tim Henman to name a few. In an open letter, McCormack wrote, "The core foundation of IMG's success has always been and will always be the representation of individual athletes, because it is they who have the power to advance sport to a new level."

William Morris Agency

With sports marketing companies collecting percentages of endorsement earnings and prize money, Maria Sharapova is clearly a golden goose when it comes to endorsements. The venerable William Morris Agency (More info: wma.com) represented movies stars such as Clark Gable and Marilyn Monroe in its heyday. Attempting to push its business envelop beyond Hollywood, the agency moved into sports marketing adding big-name tennis stars such as Serena Williams, Pete Sampras, and many future hopefuls.

SFX Sports Group

You can market just about anyone or anything when you own over 1,200 radio stations, 20-odd television stations, and 770,000 outdoor billboards, let alone over 500 of the world's elite sports professionals including Michael Jordan, Andy Roddick, and Jerry Rice. The SFX Sports Group (More info: clearchannel.com) is an independently operated talent agency owned by broadcasting conglomerate, Clear Channel Communications.

A Letter to Santa

Dear Santa:

My name is Baylee. I am six years old. I am in first grade at Sunshine Elementary. I have a big brother Alex and a little sister Alycia. I like Christmas because: It brings me joy!

I love tennis. I started playing when I was four. My parents drove me to practice and my coach Mr. Ader always made the practice so much fun.

I like reading life stories of tennis stars. I have read about Chris Evert, Monica Seles, Venus Williams, Pete Sampras, Andre Agassi, and John McEnroe. Reading about these great players makes kids like me want to learn how to play. But us kids couldn't do anything without our parents and coaches.

There needs to be a lot of help for parents and coaches so they can do a good job teaching us to play and how to be good sports. And we need to be able to get better and better without having to worry so much about winning all the time. Sometimes it's hard to find a court, Santa, so we need lots of places to play, too. Will you see what you can do for all us tennis kids out there?

What Baylee wants most for Christmas is a puppy. I also want two polo shirts – one for my Dad and the other for my favorite coach Mr. Ader. We will have cookies for you. Mom will have a nice mixed salad for the reindeer.

Merry Christmas,

Baylee

Promoters

They're quite a motley bunch, these promoters who bring tournaments and events to a community. Ranging from corporations like Silicon Valley Sports & Entertainment, which promotes a variety of sporting events, including tennis, to players-turned-entrepreneurs like Jane Stratton and Raquel Giscafré, who run a prestigious WTA tournament in San Diego, now in its 20th year.

Sports marketing companies like IMG promote the Nasdaq-100 in Miami and several other professional events, in addition to the company's million other tennis-related business interests.

Indeed, promoters come in all shapes and sizes, but it's the entrepreneurial individuals with strong community roots and a head for numbers who run this segment of the tennis industry, either working independently or within corporations. Becoming a tennis promoter is more straightforward than you might think.

Idea

Come up with an idea for an event or tournament fans will pay to watch.

Facility

Identify a facility to stage the event. Depending upon the profile of the tournament, a multi-purpose arena, private and public courts, and school and college facilities are all possibilities. Some national USTA events are held at multiple sites in close proximity to each other. Professional events have specific capacity and attendance standards that must be met. For an International Series tournament, the ATP mandates a total attendance of at least 17,500 over the six days and a 75 percent sell-out on weekends.

Players

Set a date and find players. If your event is a sanctioned tournament – ATP (More info: atptennis.com), WTA (More info: wtatour.com), or USTA (More info: usta.com) – you'll be working with these organizations to set a date and identify a pool of players you can draw from for your event. If the event is something like a college tennis exhibition, you'll probably form a committee to select a date and recruit players.

Number Crunches

Crunch your expense numbers. Prize money, facilities rental, and accommodations are some obvious expenses. You can find sanctioned tournaments with prize money as low as $10,000 for Futures series, to $3-plus million for the Tennis Masters Cup.

You must also pay a fee to the sanctioning organization. An ATP Tennis Master Series event includes a quarter million dollar fee to the ATP; an equal amount goes to the players' bonus pool; forty grand or so goes to buy rights to the tournament; and another $20,000 is needed as levy for referees and umpires. Keep in mind how and when you're required to make these payments. While prize money is payable on-site, other payments can become due as early as six months before the event.

Bring on the Stars

You want Serena Williams for your tournament in Shanghai, where the winner battles for six days to make $22,000. Fat chance? Not necessarily. Appearance fees, my friend, can make all the difference Red Alert: at many tournaments promotional considerations and fees are frowned upon by the sanctioning organization and, in many cases, there are clear rules against such perks.

Some tournaments, especially new or lower level events, may be allowed to pay appearance fees to bring in stars and boost attendance. Consider the example of an ATP International Series tournament that has the option to offer fees for promotional services. The tournament routinely pays out over $1 million, far more than the total prize money of $375,000. Appearance fees make up the lion's share of expenditures. Promoters willingly pay appearance fees. When stars commit, sponsors open their wallets and fans follow.

The "S" Word

Sponsors – selling your event to them is the true test of a promoter's mettle. Always keep in mind the reasons why companies sponsor events:

- ✓ Advertising: Corporate identification, target marketing, awareness.
- ✓ Promotion: Gains attention from trade or consumers.
- ✓ Sales: Client entertainment, sampling opportunities.
- ✓ Public Relations: The catchall phrase.

It's not uncommon for a professional tennis event to have 50 sponsors, including the all-important title sponsor and a television deal.

Now, as the promoter, all you have to do is publicize the event, sell tickets, and hold the tournament. Sounds simple, right? It can be, with good organization and planning and an experienced team. Hopefully, your tournament will make money, even when a star player calls in sick and another flies to Mexico to play a more lucrative exhibition. Welcome to the world of the big-time tennis promoter.

Player Agents

A Player Agent is a business representative who works for the player, negotiating contracts, sponsorships, endorsement deals, and other financial agreements. How well the agent manages often determines how well the player lives after his or her career is over, though few can emulate the staying power of golf legend, Arnold Palmer. More than 25 years after winning his last PGA tournament, he continued to make tens of millions of dollars in endorsements.

A growing number of agents are lawyers, while some, like Jill Smoller of the William Morris Agency, are equipped with a professional tennis background. Instead of an independent agent, many players elect to be represented by sports marketing companies such as IMG. In this case, the player is assigned an agent, also called an athlete representative.

Players with interests outside of sports often choose more than one agency. Serena Williams uses IMG for athletic representation and another William Morris Agency for her Hollywood interests. For managing a player's career, agents earn a negotiated commission that's a percentage of endorsement earnings, prize money, and appearance fees.

It takes little background or training to get into the agent business as an independent. States like California have a perfunctory law that simply requires agents to file a public disclosure form with the Secretary of State and pay a fee before engaging in business. Even junior players with good rankings will be courted by scores of agents. Courtship can happen in a hurry too – say, immediately after winning a major tournament. It makes sense to plan ahead.

When Ashley Harkleroad won the Easter Bowl's in California in 1999, the tennis world paid attention. Suddenly, Ashley, who was 14 at the time and ranked No. 1 in the United States in the Girls' 16s and 18s, received a flurry of offers for representation. Jill Smoller ultimately got the nod because of her track record with other athletes, including Pete Sampras, Pam Shriver, and Rick Fox of basketball's Los Angeles Lakers to name a few. Smoller's crossover experience in the entertainment industry was undoubtedly a plus. As Ashley was consistently winning and maintaining a high ranking, she decided to turn pro at age 15, with Smoller as her agent.

Corporate Sponsorships

While businesses pay famous players to endorse their products, they also sponsor those not yet famous in the hope that one day they'll reach celebrity status. Look at it this way: endorsement budgets are like stock investments, whereas sponsorships are investing in futures. In an earlier sponsorship arrangement with Reebok, Venus Williams, at age 12, signed a five-year, $12 million deal on the basis of her 63-0 record in the under 12s.

Sponsorship implies that the company pays a portion of training expenses, while endorsement suggests that the player is a company spokesperson or business representative. A company might sponsor many promising athletes, but hire only one or two more famous players as spokespersons.

It's common for a Nike or Reebok to offer $100,000 to $200,000 annual sponsorship deals to a good number of promising juniors. Before accepting a sponsorship deal, juniors are advised to check how the deal will affect amateur status, should the junior choose to continue playing amateur tournaments or apply for college scholarships.

Ultimately, players earn sponsorships to help businesses get their brands in front of as many consumer eyeballs as possible, in stadiums and on television. Sponsors also make one-match deals with low-ranked players who wear temporary patches bearing the sponsors' logos when playing in early round matches of televised tournaments.

Endorsements

A company pays a famous player a fee for making a public endorsement of its products. Beyond wearing the company's shoes, apparel, and logos, the player may be contracted to attend corporate functions, appear in photo shoots and commercials, support related corporate ventures, and lend his name to a new product.

Ever wonder why a sneaker with $11 worth of materials costs you $80? Here's the scoop from Nike:

Sneaker Economics 101

STEP 1:

Materials	$11
Factory cost	$6
Factory profit	$1
Nike pays factory	$18

STEP 2:

Shoe cost	$18
Nike cost: R&D to develop new shoes, ***endorsements***, and television commercials	$17
Nike taxes	$1.50
Nike net profits	$2.50

STEP 3:

Product cost	$39
Retailer cost: Sales people, rent	$38
Taxes	$1
Retailer net profit	$2
COST TO CONSUMER	$80

* Source: Nike

No player is more endorsement-savvy than hall-of-famer, Jack Kramer. Now in his eighties, Kramer nonetheless pulls in his two-and-half percent or so from every Jack Kramer racket sold by Wilson Sporting Goods, a deal said to have netted him over $13 million so far. More than five decades after winning the US Championships, you can find the new Limited Edition Jack Kramer racket in stores and at auctions selling for hundreds of dollars.

Endorsement contracts vary. Corporations are interested in phenoms who can move products by virtue of a fickle mix of on-court performance, off-court antics and, for the younger crowd, aura.

The Williams sisters can probably justify every cent of the millions they earn from endorsements. They attract a sell-out crowd even in Timbaktu; their television commercials are a hit; magazines with the sisters on the covers routinely sell out, not to mention the booming business in calendars, videos, and accessories.

When Reebok agreed to a five-year contract with Venus Williams that guaranteed her $8 million per year, they had already projected huge sales of shoes and other Reebok products and whatever else they make, based on Venus's on-court achievements and her Cinderella aura.

After top endorsers like Andre Agassi, Pete Sampras, Andy Roddick, Maria Sharapova, and Venus and Serena Williams, come the next tier of players like Lindsay Davenport and Jennifer Capriati, who also make a few million each in endorsements. The players who make up the rest of the top 30 roster will likely earn several hundred thousand dollars in endorsements. Most pros get free rackets and gear, but it is rare for someone outside the top 30 to make significant money from endorsements.

Interestingly, a variety of organizations and individuals make up the inside world of endorsements. You have the player and her immediate entourage, including coach and family members. Then there's the player agent or athlete rep from the player's sports marketing company. And finally, you have to have lawyers and accountants, Price Waterhouse Coopers, for example, to pour over the fine print.

Then you have a business like Burns Sports, which maintains a database of agents and their sports celebrity clients. Corporations call Burns when they need a sports celebrity for their ad campaigns. The folks at Burns find an appropriate match for these corporate clients. ATP and WTA management are also on the bandwagon, playing a larger role in marketing their respective tours to corporations and thus expanding the endorsement base for all professional players.

Endorsements are a big-time business because we gladly part with a few dollars more to pick up an Roger Federer Dri-Fit Polo for ourselves and a Serena-21 racket for the little one. Who knows, one day *your* tennis kid may be on the endorsement list, motivating millions of buyers.

Select References

1. Nicole den Duyn. *Game Sense: It's time to play*. Vol. 19, No. 4, 1997. Australian Sports Coach.

2. Paul Webb and Cary Thompson. *Developing Thinking Players: Game Sense in Coaching and Teaching.* 1999. PDHPE Teachers Association Conference.

3. E Paul Roetert, Gladys E Garrett, Scott W Brown and David N Carnalone. *Performance Profiles of Nationally Ranked Junior Tennis Players.* Vol. 6, No. 4, 1992. Journal of Applied Sport Science Research.

4. E Paul Roetert, Scott W Brown, Patricia A Piorkowski and Ronald B Woods. *Fitness Comparison Among Three Different Levels of Elite Tennis Players.* Vol 10, No. 3, 1996. Journal of Strength and Conditioning Research.

5. Lori Parsons and Margaret Jones. *Development of Speed, Agility and Quickness for Tennis Athletes.* Vol. 20, No. 3, 1998. Strength and Conditioning.

Index

Acknowledgments

Moxie. I always wanted to use this word in my book. Now that I've finally found a place for it, I'm getting over this little writer's obsession and moving on to the real deal. My expression of gratitude to people without whose support this work would simply be an incomplete Word document, occupying space on my computer's hard drive. Their generosity of time and expertise benefited me and, through this work, will benefit you and your tennis kid(s).

My sincere thanks to:

- Amy Binder, WTA Tour
- Babette Pluim, President, Society for Tennis Medicine and Science
- Bob Larson, Publisher, TennisNews.com
- Bob Williams, President, Burns Sports & Celebrities, Inc.
- Brent Zeller, Tennis Pro, EffortlessTennis.com
- Carol Shaner, Executive Vice President, United States Tennis Court and Track Builders Association, and author of Tennis Courts.
- Casey Angle, Director of Communications, Intercollegiate Tennis Association
- Cathy Scheder, Manager Learning Resources, American Camping Association
- Charles Hoeveler, President, US Sports and Specialty Camps
- Chris Decker, Tennis Pro, Universal Tennis Academy
- Chris & Jennifer Yoder, Head Pros, Yoder Tennis
- Crawford Lindsey, Master Racquet Technician, United States Racquet Stringers Association and co-author of The Physics and Technology of Tennis
- Dan O'Connell, Development Officer, International Tennis Federation
- Darren Potkey, Player Development, USTA/Southern California Section
- Dr. Adam Naylor, Sports Psychology Coach, Boston University Athletic Enhancement Center
- Dr. Jim Taylor, Alpine/Taylor Consulting and author of Positive Pushing.
- Greg Moran, Head Tennis Pro, Four Seasons Racquet Club
- Greg Raven, Master Racquet Technician, United States Racquet Stringers Association

- Hilary Somers, Community Tennis, USTA/Northern California Section
- Jack Broudy, President, Grail Sports Inc.
- Jay Hacker, Chairperson, Junior Ranking Committee, United States Tennis Association
- Janice Bell, IMG Academies; Jennifer Wolfe and Linda Dozoretz
- Jeff Drock, Strength and Conditioning Coach
- Jill Smoller, Vice President, William Morris Agency
- Joe Dinoffer, President, Oncourt Offcourt, Inc.
- Kat Anderson and Mark Young, International Tennis Hall of Fame
- Keith Adams, Head Pro, Your Advantage Tennis
- Lynn Miller, Varsity Tennis Coach, Wheaton College
- Peggy Edwards, Director – Marketing & Communications, Professional Tennis Registry
- Rich Maizel, Managing Partner, New Shrewsbury Racquet Club
- Roger Darrohn, Director of Operations, Peter Burwash International
- Sean Brawley, Athletic Performance Consultant and former player on the ATP tour
- Shannon Grossi, TIA Executive Assistant, Tennis Industry Association
- Shawna Riley, Editor, ADDvantage magazine, United States Professional Tennis Association

I thank Dale Berra, Dr. Alan Goldberg, Dr Jani Pallis, Herbert Cheyette, Jeff Tarango, Jennifer Ryan, Rebecca Milot-Bradford, Retesha Thadison, Rick Wolff, Stacy Allison, and Tony Lance for help with permissions and releases. Appreciate the assistance I received from the Public Relations, Communications, and Publications staffs of various tennis organizations mentioned in the book.

Special thanks to Pamela Garrett for her brilliant editing and counsel; Uday Kumar for diligent work with permissions & reviews; R. Christian Anderson for his creative cover; Bill Carson for updating the cover; and to Maureen Malliaras for her excellent assistance in coordinating the project.

To Neel K. and Andrew L., two kids who gave up quite a few summer days flagging and sorting my writing. I owe you much more than the ice cream sundae.

Aces to you all,
Keith Kattan

Make Your Next Tennis Event A Huge Success

Made in the USA
San Bernardino, CA
19 August 2013